CARD PLAY
FUNDAMENTALS

by
Easley Blackwood
and
Keith Hanson

**Published by
Devyn Press, Inc.
Louisville, Kentucky**

Cover by Bonnie Baron Pollack

Printed in the United States of America.

Devyn Press, Inc.
151 Thierman Lane
Louisville, KY 40207

ISBN 0-910791-46-5

INTRODUCTION

This book is designed to help you improve your bridge card play. While you are growing, keep in mind three things:

1. Have patience — bridge is a game of experience. Skill will improve with time and study.
2. Have fun — bridge is an impossible game to play perfectly. Don't get uptight. Relax and enjoy yourself.
3. Be a good partner — the most important single skill any bridge player can possess is to be a good partner.

The variables will lead to play and bidding problems where the best play will inevitably work out poorly on occasion. Demonstrate a positive friendly attitude and you will

A. Get better scores
B. Have more fun
C. Be in high demand as a partner.

GOOD LUCK

CONTENTS

Chapter 1

DECLARER PLAY FUNDAMENTALS I

SURE TRICKS

Understanding how to play a bridge hand begins with the concept of sure tricks. A sure trick is a trick which can be won without losing the lead. Inspect each suit in the following practice hands and count the available sure tricks:

1. *Dummy*
   ♠ A 9 4
   ♡ A 8 7 6
   ♢ 5 3 2
   ♣ K 6 3

   You
   ♠ K 8 3
   ♡ K 4
   ♢ A 8 7 6 4
   ♣ A Q 7

2. *Dummy*
   ♠ A 8 3 2
   ♡ A K 9
   ♢ A K 7
   ♣ K 6 4

   You
   ♠ 7 5 4
   ♡ Q 5 2
   ♢ Q 8 3
   ♣ A 7 5 2

3. *Dummy*
    ♠ A K Q J 10
    ♡ A K Q
    ◇ 9 5 4
    ♣ A 2

    You
    ♠ 7 5 2
    ♡ 10 4 3
    ◇ A 8 3
    ♣ K Q J 9

4. *Dummy*
    ♠ J 10 5
    ♡ K 8 4
    ◇ K J 7
    ♣ Q J 4 3

    You
    ♠ K Q 6
    ♡ Q J 7 2
    ◇ Q 10 3
    ♣ K 7 5

Answers:

1. You have eight sure tricks: two spades, two hearts, one diamond and three clubs.
2. You have nine sure tricks: one spade, three hearts, three diamonds, and two clubs.
3. You have thirteen sure tricks: five spades, three hearts, one diamond and four clubs.
4. You have zero sure tricks: on this hand you must develop tricks.

DEVELOPING EXTRA TRICKS

In most bridge hands you will not have enough sure tricks to succeed in your contract. It will be necessary to develop extra tricks. There are three primary methods of developing new tricks:

A. Promoting Honor Cards
B. Establishing Long Suits
C. Finessing

When developing extra tricks, keep in mind the following:

1. Know the number of tricks needed to make your contract. Develop additional tricks if they are needed.
2. Develop the extra tricks necessary to make your contract before cashing your sure tricks.
3. Do not fear giving up the lead.

Promoting Honor Cards

Lower ranking honor cards can be promoted into sure tricks by forcing higher ranking cards to be played.

1. *North*
   (dummy)
   ♡ Q J 9

   South
   ♡ K 7 5

2. *North*
   (dummy)
   ♡ Q 10 4 3

   South
   ♡ J 9 7 2

In Hand 1 by leading an honor to force out the ace, you promote two extra tricks.

In Hand 2 by leading one of your high cards to force out the ace or king, you begin the promotion process. By doing it a second time, you will promote two extra tricks.

Count your sure tricks and tricks that can be developed by honor promotion in the following practice hands:

1. *Dummy*
    ♠ A K Q
    ♡ K 9 7 6
    ◇ 5 4 2
    ♣ K 10 6

    You
    ♠ 8 3
    ♡ A 5 3
    ◇ K Q J 10
    ♣ A Q J 3

2. *Dummy*
    ♠ A 9 8
    ♡ J 5 4
    ◇ A 7 2
    ♣ K 6 4 2

    You
    ♠ K 7 3
    ♡ Q 10 9 6
    ◇ K 5
    ♣ A 8 5 3

3. *Dummy*
    ♠ 9 7 6
    ♡ A 8 4 3
    ◇ 8 6 2
    ♣ A K 10

    You
    ♠ A K 4
    ♡ K 7 2
    ◇ Q J 10 9
    ♣ Q 8 4

4. *Dummy*
    ♠ A 9 2
    ♡ K Q 8
    ◇ A Q 6
    ♣ Q J 10 9

    You
    ♠ K Q 6
    ♡ A 6 5
    ◇ K 5 3
    ♣ 9 8 4 2

Answers:

1. You have nine sure tricks: three spades, two hearts and four clubs. You have three promotable diamond tricks.
2. You have six sure tricks: two each in spades, diamonds and clubs. You have two promotable heart tricks.
3. You have seven sure tricks: two spades, two hearts and three clubs. You have two promotable diamond tricks.
4. You have nine sure tricks: three each in spades, hearts and diamonds. You have two promotable club tricks.

Establishing Long Suits

A second method to develop extra tricks is by establishing long suits. To develop long suits into additional tricks, you must hold a five-card suit in one hand or seven or more cards in the suit between your hand and dummy. Long suits should be established early, before cashing your sure tricks.

Play the following practice hands. In each case the contract is 3 NT and the opening lead is the ♡2. Which suit should you as declarer play first? Remember you need nine tricks.

1. *Dummy*
   ♠ A 8 4
   ♡ A 6 5
   ◇ A 9 2
   ♣ A 7 6 4

   You
   ♠ K Q 9
   ♡ K 7 3
   ◇ K 4 3
   ♣ 9 5 3 2

2. *Dummy*
   ♠ K 9
   ♡ A 8
   ◇ A 7 6 5 4 2
   ♣ A 9 7

   You
   ♠ A 8 6 4 2
   ♡ K Q 3
   ◇ 10 8
   ♣ K 6 5

3. *Dummy*
   ♠ A 9
   ♡ K 4 3
   ◇ K 10 2
   ♣ J 9 4 3 2

   You
   ♠ K 8 3
   ♡ A 9 5
   ◇ A Q 7
   ♣ 10 7 6 5

4. *Dummy*
   ♠ K Q 9
   ♡ 7 5 4
   ◇ A 8 4 2
   ♣ A Q 10

   You
   ♠ A 10 3
   ♡ A 9 2
   ◇ K 7 6 3
   ♣ K 8 4

Answers:

1. You have eight sure tricks: three spades, two hearts, two diamonds and one club. Play clubs in the hope of developing a ninth trick.
2. Again you have eight sure tricks: two spades, three hearts, one diamond and two clubs. The longest combined suit between your hand and dummy is diamonds. Play diamonds.
3. You have seven sure tricks: two spades, two hearts and three diamonds. You need two more tricks and the only hope is to develop the club suit. Play those anemic clubs!
4. You have nine sure tricks: three spades, one heart, two diamonds and three clubs. Lucky you. On this hand you have enough sure tricks for your contract and should simply cash them.

Finessing

Finessing is a basic card-play technique and is another method to develop extra tricks.

A finesse is an attempt to trap a missing honor card held by a defender by forcing him to play before you decide whether to play a high card or a lower card. Finesses are usually begun by leading from one hand up to broken honor strength in the other hand. You hope to gain a positional advantage by playing after the defender holding the hoped for honor(s).

Some finessing positions are

A Q	K J 10	K 8	A 5 4
4 3	8 7 6	9 4	Q J 10

Finesses are:

1. 50% to win but are not a gamble. You are risking nothing as you are attempting to win an extra trick you otherwise would not win.
2. Not always an attempt to win all the tricks. They are an attempt to win the maximum possible.
3. A hope that a certain card is favorably located.

Basic Finesses

Play the following card combinations. Assume the bottom hand (South) is you, the declarer. The top hand (North) is dummy. Answer these four questions for each card combination.

1. What card should you lead from the South hand?
2. What key card are you finessing West for?
3. How many tricks will you win if West has the key card?
4. Assume West plays low. What card do you play from dummy?

1. *North*
   A Q

   South
   3 2

2. *South*
   K 4

   South
   6 5

3. *North*
   A 7 4

   South
   Q J 10

4. *North*
   A Q 10

   South
   J 9 8

5. *North*
   K Q 5

   South
   8 6 3

6. *North*
   A 7 6 2

   South
   Q J 10 9

7. *North*
   A K J 10

   South
   7 6 5

8. *North*
   A Q J

   South
   6 3 2

9. *North*
   A J 4

   South
   K 5 2

10. *North*
    K J 10

    South
    7 5 2

Answers:

1. Lead the two. Finesse West for the king. You will win two tricks. Play the queen.
2. Lead the five. Finesse West for the ace. You will win one trick. Play the king.
3. Lead the queen. Finesse West for the king. You will win three tricks. Play the four.
4. Lead the jack. Finesse West for the king. You will win three tricks. Play the ten.
5. Lead the three. Finesse West for the ace. You will win two tricks. Play the king or queen. You will need another entry to the South hand to repeat this finesse.
6. Lead any card. Finesse West for the king. You will win four tricks. Play the two.
7. Lead the five. Finesse West for the queen. You will win four tricks. Play the jack or ten. You will need another entry to the South hand to repeat this finesse.
8. Lead the two. Finesse West for the king. You will win three tricks. Play the queen or jack. You will need another entry to the South hand to repeat this finesse.
9. Lead the two. Finesse West for the queen. You will win three tricks. Play the jack.
10. Lead the two. Finesse West for the queen. You will win two tricks. Play the jack or ten. You will need another entry to the South hand to repeat this finesse.

PLANNING A NOTRUMP CONTRACT

Always pause before playing to the first trick. Study the dummy and make an overall plan for the hand.

Notrump contracts are usually a race between the declarer and the defenders to establish and win tricks with their side's long suit. Remember the defenders have the advantage of the opening lead.

Steps in notrump planning:

a) Count sure winners — compare with the contract — plan to develop extra tricks if needed
b) Keep entries in the hand holding the long suit
c) Control the opponents' long suit (hold-up play)
d) Establish your long suit (almost always)

Remember, to establish your long suit, you will usually have to lose one or more tricks. **DON'T BE AFRAID TO LOSE THE LEAD.** Do it early, before cashing your sure tricks.

Count Winners — Compare With the Contract — Develop Extra Tricks

```
                    ♠ K 7 5
                    ♡ 7 3 2
                    ♢ Q 8 7 6
                    ♣ 4 3 2
    ♠ Q J 10 9               ♠ 8 6 2
    ♡ 10 9 8          N      ♡ Q J 6 5
    ♢ A 3 2        W   E     ♢ 9 5
    ♣ J 9 8          S       ♣ Q 10 7 6
                    ♠ A 4 3
                    ♡ A K 4
                    ♢ K J 10 4
                    ♣ A K 5
```

Contract: 3 NT
Opening Lead: ♠Q

Count the sure winners — six. Compare with the contract — you need nine tricks. Plan to develop extra tricks. Note that you can develop three extra diamond tricks. Plan to lead diamond honors until the ace is played. It would be incorrect to cash your sure tricks first as this would establish winners for the defenders. You have nothing to fear by losing the lead.

Keep Entries in the Hand Holding the Long Suit

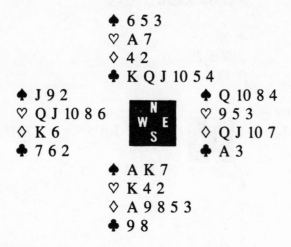

```
              ♠ 6 5 3
              ♡ A 7
              ◇ 4 2
              ♣ K Q J 10 5 4
♠ J 9 2                        ♠ Q 10 8 4
♡ Q J 10 8 6      N            ♡ 9 5 3
◇ K 6           W   E          ◇ Q J 10 7
♣ 7 6 2           S            ♣ A 3
              ♠ A K 7
              ♡ K 4 2
              ◇ A 9 8 5 3
              ♣ 9 8
```

Contract: 3 NT
Opening Lead: ♡Q

a) Count your sure winners — five. Compare with the contract — you need nine tricks. Plan to develop extra tricks. After forcing out the ♣A, you will have five extra club tricks.

b) Keep entries in the hand holding the long suit. You have to be careful in playing to the first trick. You must save the ♡A — the only entry to North's long club suit. Win the first trick with the ♡K, play clubs and you will easily win ten tricks.

Control the Opponents' Suit — The Hold Up Play

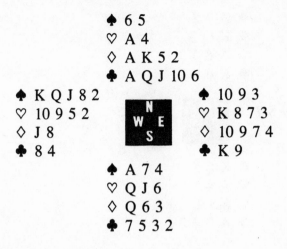

```
                    ♠ 6 5
                    ♡ A 4
                    ◇ A K 5 2
                    ♣ A Q J 10 6
  ♠ K Q J 8 2                    ♠ 10 9 3
  ♡ 10 9 5 2          N          ♡ K 8 7 3
  ◇ J 8            W     E        ◇ 10 9 7 4
  ♣ 8 4               S          ♣ K 9
                    ♠ A 7 4
                    ♡ Q J 6
                    ◇ Q 6 3
                    ♣ 7 5 3 2
```

Contract: 3 NT
Opening Lead: ♠K

a) Count your sure winners — six. Compare with the contract — you need nine tricks. Plan to develop extra tricks. You can develop three or four extra club tricks depending on who has the ♣K. You plan to finesse against West.

b) Keep entries in the hand holding the long suit — no problem, North has three aces and a king as entries.

c) Control the opponents' long suit. The danger is that the opponents may win the ♣K and cash enough spade tricks to defeat your contract. By holding up your ♠A until the third lead — that is, by not winning either the first or the second spade trick — you exhaust East of spades. Win the third spade and take the club finesse. It loses but East has no more spades and you make 3 NT.

Establish Your Long Suit

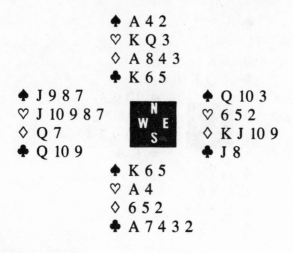

```
              ♠ A 4 2
              ♡ K Q 3
              ◇ A 8 4 3
              ♣ K 6 5
♠ J 9 8 7                    ♠ Q 10 3
♡ J 10 9 8 7      N          ♡ 6 5 2
◇ Q 7          W     E       ◇ K J 10 9
♣ Q 10 9          S          ♣ J 8
              ♠ K 6 5
              ♡ A 4
              ◇ 6 5 2
              ♣ A 7 4 3 2
```

Contract: 3 NT
Opening Lead: ♡ J

a) Count your sure winners — eight. Compare with the contract — you need nine tricks. Plan to develop extra tricks — as in most notrump hands, you should attack your long suit.

b) Keep entries in the hand holding the long suit — no problem here. You have the ♠ K.

c) Control the opponents' suit — again no problem — you have the ♡ A, ♡ K and ♡ Q. Lead the ♣ K and ♣ A and concede a club to the defenders. Your ♣ 7 and ♣ 4 are now established. You make 3 NT with an overtrick.

PLANNING A TRUMP CONTRACT

As in notrump contracts, pause and study the dummy before playing to the first trick. There are four steps in planning the play of a trump contract:

a. **Count** the trump winners you will have with a normal division
b. **Count** sure side suit winners (as in notrump)
c. **Examine** each suit for potential additional tricks
d. **Plan** in which order to play the suits

Dummy
♠ A 6 4 2
♥ K 7 5
◇ A Q
♣ 8 6 4 3

You
♠ K 3
♥ A 9 6 4 3 2
◇ 9 7 5
♣ K 5

EXAMPLE — You are in 4♥ with the ♠10 lead. Plan the play.

ORIGINAL COUNT
Spades   = 2 sure tricks
Hearts   = 5 estimated tricks [four (trumps) missing cards are most likely to divide 3-1]
Diamonds = 1 sure trick
Clubs   = 0 sure tricks
Total   = 8

POTENTIAL ADDITIONAL TRICKS
Spades   = 0
Hearts   = 1 (suit may divide 2-2)
Diamonds = 2 (one by finessing the queen, one by ruffing the third diamond in dummy)
Clubs   = 1 (by leading from dummy toward the king)
Total   = 4 possible extra tricks

YOUR PLAN

Take the diamond finesse immediately. Later ruff your third diamond with dummy's ♡5. Then play the ♡A and ♡K. Lead a club towards the king. You could make twelve tricks with good fortune or go down with bad luck.

A second example for playing trump contracts.

Dummy
♠ Q 7 5
♡ 10 7 5 2
♢ 9 4
♣ A K J 5

You
♠ K J 8 4 3
♡ K Q
♢ A K 2
♣ 9 4 2

ANOTHER EXAMPLE — You are in 4♠ with the ♢Q lead. Plan the play.

ORIGINAL COUNT

Spades	= 4 estimated tricks (five trumps), missing cards are most likely to divide 3-2.
Hearts	= 0 sure tricks
Diamonds	= 2 sure tricks
Clubs	= 2 sure tricks
Total	= 8

POTENTIAL ADDITIONAL TRICKS

Spades	= 0
Hearts	= 1 (by honor promotion)
Diamonds	= 1 (by ruffing the ♢2 in dummy)
Clubs	= 1 (by finessing the ♣J)
Total	= 3 possible extra tricks

YOUR PLAN

Play the ♢A and ♢K. Ruff your ♢2 with dummy's ♠5. Play the ♠Q and continue drawing trumps when you regain the lead. Later lead a heart honor to promote a certain extra trick. Then lead a club to dummy's jack for a finesse. You could win as few as eight tricks or as many as eleven.

Three Primary Methods of Playing Suit Contracts

a. Draw the opponents' trumps immediately (most common)
b. Hands where trump drawing must be postponed

1. Until dummy's trumps are used for ruffing
2. Until an early discard is taken
3. Until a side suit is established
4. Until a finesse is taken

c. Hands where trumps are never drawn (cross-ruff which is rare)

Again, do not be afraid to lose a trick or surrender the lead.

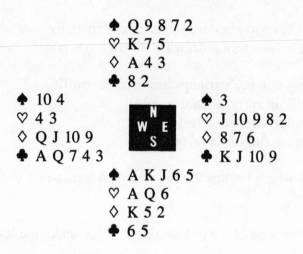

♠ Q 9 8 7 2
♡ K 7 5
♢ A 4 3
♣ 8 2

♠ 10 4
♡ 4 3
♢ Q J 10 9
♣ A Q 7 4 3

♠ 3
♡ J 10 9 8 2
♢ 8 7 6
♣ K J 10 9

♠ A K J 6 5
♡ A Q 6
♢ K 5 2
♣ 6 5

Contract: 4 ♠
Opening Lead: ♢ Q

You count five sure trump tricks as well as three top hearts and two top diamonds. This is the most common type of trump contract. Simply draw trumps (in this case two rounds) and take your ten tricks. Note if you fool around and play hearts before drawing trumps, West will trump the third heart and you will go down. The most common first step in playing a trump contract is to draw trumps.

Postpone Drawing Trumps —
Use Dummy's Trumps for Ruffing

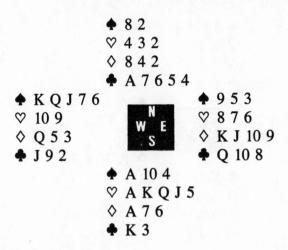

♠ 8 2
♡ 4 3 2
◊ 8 4 2
♣ A 7 6 5 4

♠ K Q J 7 6   ♠ 9 5 3
♡ 10 9   ♡ 8 7 6
◊ Q 5 3   ◊ K J 10 9
♣ J 9 2   ♣ Q 10 8

♠ A 10 4
♡ A K Q J 5
◊ A 7 6
♣ K 3

Contract: 4♡
Opening Lead: ♠K

You estimate five trump tricks (five missing cards are over
96% to break 3-2 or 4-1). Add one sure spade trick, one sure
diamond trick and two sure club tricks. You need one more
trick. If you draw trumps immediately, you will be down one.
Plan instead to ruff your third spade in dummy. Win the ♠A
and immediately return a spade. Upon regaining the lead, ruff
your ♠10 with dummy's ♡2. Then draw trumps and make
ten tricks. Extra tricks often can be created by ruffing in the
short hand (usually dummy). Ruffing in the long trump hand
does not create extra tricks and should be avoided. These long
trumps are already tricks.

Postpone Drawing Trumps —
Take an Early Discard

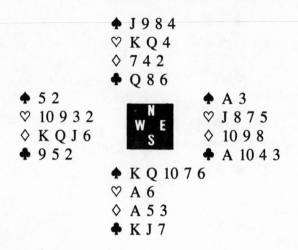

♠ J 9 8 4
♡ K Q 4
◇ 7 4 2
♣ Q 8 6

♠ 5 2
♡ 10 9 3 2
◇ K Q J 6
♣ 9 5 2

♠ A 3
♡ J 8 7 5
◇ 10 9 8
♣ A 10 4 3

♠ K Q 10 7 6
♡ A 6
◇ A 5 3
♣ K J 7

Contract: 4 ♠
Opening Lead: ◇ K

You count four trump tricks as you are missing only the ace.
Add three sure heart tricks, one sure diamond trick, and two
potential club tricks (by forcing out the ace). Your trick total
is ten. The problem is that if you surrender the lead immediately
by playing trumps, you have four fast losers (♠A, two
diamonds, ♣A). The solution is to postpone drawing trumps
and play the ♡A, ♡K, ♡Q instead. On the ♡Q, discard a
diamond loser. You now have only one diamond loser remaining in your hand. You then begin the trump pulling process
and make your 4 ♠ contract. Delay drawing trumps when you
have too many quick losers and need to take an early discard.

Postpone Drawing Trumps —
Establish a Side Suit

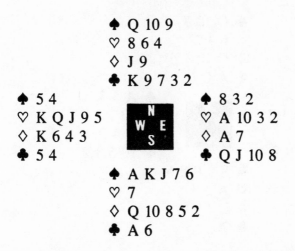

```
              ♠ Q 10 9
              ♡ 8 6 4
              ◇ J 9
              ♣ K 9 7 3 2
  ♠ 5 4                      ♠ 8 3 2
  ♡ K Q J 9 5                ♡ A 10 3 2
  ◇ K 6 4 3                  ◇ A 7
  ♣ 5 4                      ♣ Q J 10 8
              ♠ A K J 7 6
              ♡ 7
              ◇ Q 10 8 5 2
              ♣ A 6
```

Contract: 4 ♠
Opening Lead: ♡ K

You have five sure trump tricks and two sure club tricks.
The diamond suit has three potential tricks. When playing in
a trump contract and you must develop tricks in a side suit,
you have to be careful that you don't run out of trumps before
your side suit is established. Often you will delay drawing
trumps so that you can trump the opponents' high cards in dummy rather than be forced to trump in your hand. Ruff the second heart and immediately attack diamonds. Force out the
defenders' ◇ A and ◇ K (developing your Q108 into winners).
If the opponents continue hearts, ruff the third round in your
hand but ruff the fourth round in dummy. If you had drawn
trumps before establishing the diamonds, you would go set.
You could ruff the third round of hearts when the defenders
win one of their diamond honors, but then you would be out
of trumps and when the opponents win their other diamond
honor they would cash some hearts. When you have to develop
a side suit, make sure you can control the hand if you draw
trumps.

Postpone Drawing Trumps —
Take a Finesse

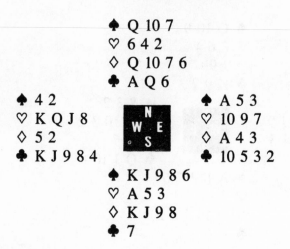

♠ Q 10 7
♡ 6 4 2
◇ Q 10 7 6
♣ A Q 6

♠ 4 2
♡ K Q J 8
◇ 5 2
♣ K J 9 8 4

♠ A 5 3
♡ 10 9 7
◇ A 4 3
♣ 10 5 3 2

♠ K J 9 8 6
♡ A 5 3
◇ K J 9 8
♣ 7

Contract: 4♠
Opening Lead: ♡K

You have four eventual trump tricks, one sure heart trick, one sure club trick, and three readily-establishable diamond tricks. You need one additional trick and the only legitimate possibility of an extra trick is in clubs. You must take an immediate club finesse in order to discard a heart loser. If the finesse fails you are down two, a small price to pay for the chance of making your contract. Playing trumps immediately would result in a sure down one.

Never Draw Trumps —
Cross-Ruff

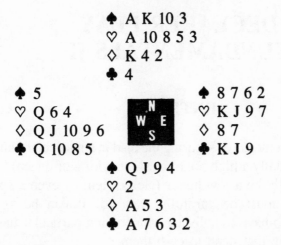

```
              ♠ A K 10 3
              ♡ A 10 8 5 3
              ◊ K 4 2
              ♣ 4
♠ 5                          ♠ 8 7 6 2
♡ Q 6 4          N           ♡ K J 9 7
◊ Q J 10 9 6   W   E         ◊ 8 7
♣ Q 10 8 5       S           ♣ K J 9
              ♠ Q J 9 4
              ♡ 2
              ◊ A 5 3
              ♣ A 7 6 3 2
```

Contract: 6♠
Opening Lead: ◊ Q

You have four sure trump tricks, one sure heart trick, two sure diamond tricks and one sure club trick. You will have only eight tricks if you draw trumps but twelve if you can make all your trumps separately by cross-ruffing.

Usual cross-ruff technique:

1. If both hands have a singleton or void, consider a cross-ruff
2. Cash your side suit winners immediately (on the above hand, the ◊A and ◊K are side suit winners)
3. You must take a chance and ruff early with low trumps when necessary (ruff early with the three in dummy and the four in your hand on the above hand)

Win the ◊A and ◊K. Cross-ruff clubs and hearts to make all your trumps.

REMEMBER, cross-ruff hands are rare.

Chapter 2

DECLARER PLAY FUNDAMENTALS II

ENTRIES

An entry is a means of securing the lead in a particular hand. An entry is usually a high honor card (ace, king or queen) but can occasionally be a low honor (jack or ten) or even a spot card. Entries must be carefully watched. It can be very discouraging to have established winners in a particular hand and no entry in that hand to cash them.

Entries Guidelines

1. Try to keep entries in both hands in case of an unexpected need
2. Preserve entries in the weak hand (usually dummy)
3. Try to keep a flexible entry position in the trump suit if both hands hold length. For example, your trumps are:

> *Dummy*
> Q J 10 8 6
>
> *You*
> A K 9 7 2

You wish to draw trumps and are not sure where you may later need entries. It would be poor technique to cash the AK leaving dummy with all the entries. Better to play the ace and then the two to the queen. This leaves K97 opposite J108 — a flexible position.

Entries

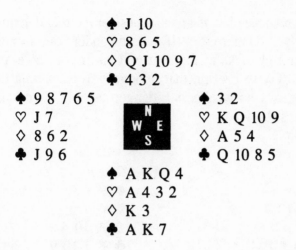

♠ J 10
♡ 8 6 5
◇ Q J 10 9 7
♣ 4 3 2

♠ 9 8 7 6 5
♡ J 7
◇ 8 6 2
♣ J 9 6

♠ 3 2
♡ K Q 10 9
◇ A 5 4
♣ Q 10 8 5

♠ A K Q 4
♡ A 4 3 2
◇ K 3
♣ A K 7

Contract: 3 NT
Opening Lead: ♠9

You pause to count your sure tricks and plan the play. The
sure tricks: seven (four spades, one heart and two clubs). The
diamond suit offers four potential tricks. You notice that dummy is very weak. Where is the entry to the long diamonds if
the defenders hold up the ◇ A one round? The ♠ J is the only
potential entry. Win the first trick with the ♠ Q. Now play the
◇ K and continue diamonds. The ♠ 4 can later be led to dummy's jack as an entry to cash the winning diamonds. You win
eleven tricks. If you had carelessly won the first trick with the
♠ 10, you would be down one.

THE DANGER HAND

When you plan the play of a hand, consider if either defender is particularly "dangerous." If one defender can run an established suit or make a shift that will harm you, he is the danger hand. Try to prevent that opponent from gaining the lead. Frequently your weakness is dangerous only if a certain defender gains the lead.

Two examples:

A. *Dummy*
   ♠ 8 6 4
   ♡ K J 10 9
   ◊ 9 5
   ♣ A Q J 4

   Declarer (You)
   ♠ K 7 5
   ♡ A 8 7 6
   ◊ A K 4
   ♣ K 10 4

Contact: 4 ♡
Opening Lead: ◊ Q

B. *Dummy*
   ♠ 9 4 3
   ♡ A 7 6
   ◊ A 10 4
   ♣ K J 10 9

   Declarer (You)
   ♠ A 7 2
   ♡ K 8 3
   ◊ K Q 9
   ♣ A 6 4 3

Contact: 3 NT
Opening Lead: ♠ K

Example A — You have at least ten winners (three or four hearts depending on whether you guess the ♡ Q, two diamonds, a diamond ruff and four clubs). The danger is that East might gain the lead and push a spade through your king. To avoid this possibility you should finesse East for the ♡ Q to protect your ♠ K from attack. East is the danger hand.

Example B — West leads a spade and you refuse to win the ace (hold up) until the third round. East shows out on the third spade. West has established two spade winners and is the danger hand. You should play the ace and another club, finessing West for the queen if it has not appeared.

The Danger Hand

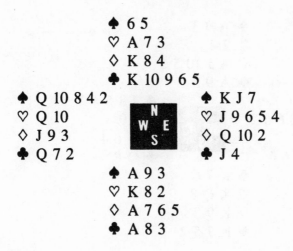

```
            ♠ 6 5
            ♡ A 7 3
            ◇ K 8 4
            ♣ K 10 9 6 5
♠ Q 10 8 4 2              ♠ K J 7
♡ Q 10          N        ♡ J 9 6 5 4
◇ J 9 3       W   E      ◇ Q 10 2
♣ Q 7 2          S       ♣ J 4
            ♠ A 9 3
            ♡ K 8 2
            ◇ A 7 6 5
            ♣ A 8 3
```

Contract: 3 NT
Opening Lead: ♠4

   You routinely hold up your ♠A until the third round. You
have seven sure winners and must develop the club suit.
You also must keep West from winning the lead as he has two
good spades to cash. You should play the ace and a low club
to the nine in dummy. East will win and can do you no harm.
If West has the QJ and another club, the hand cannot be made.

The Danger Hand

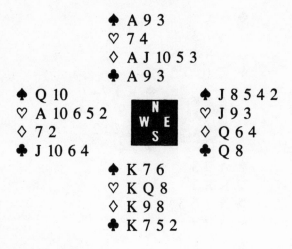

♠ A 9 3
♡ 7 4
◊ A J 10 5 3
♣ A 9 3

♠ Q 10
♡ A 10 6 5 2
◊ 7 2
♣ J 10 6 4

♠ J 8 5 4 2
♡ J 9 3
◊ Q 6 4
♣ Q 8

♠ K 7 6
♡ K Q 8
◊ K 9 8
♣ K 7 5 2

Contract: 3 NT
Opening Lead: ♡5

East plays the jack and you win the king. You have seven sure tricks (two in each suit plus the one already taken in hearts) and must develop diamonds. If East gains the lead he will return a heart through your remaining Q8 and you will go down. Enter dummy with a black ace and lead the ◊ J. If this finesse loses to West, the contract is still safe as West can do no harm. On the actual hand, you will win ten tricks.

SAFETY PLAY

A safety play is a play by the declarer which ensures or maximizes the chance to take at least a specific number of tricks in a suit and may sacrifice the possibility of taking a greater number of tricks in that suit. A safety play is generally the play of a particular suit in such a manner as to guard against an unusually bad break. It guarantees or improves the chance of making the contract at the possible sacrifice of one or more overtricks.

Safety plays that sacrifice a possible overtrick are most frequently used in rubber bridge, Chicago or team games. They are rare in matchpoints where overtricks are critically important.

Safety plays are like an insurance policy. They improve chances for or guarantee the success of the contract.

Safety Play

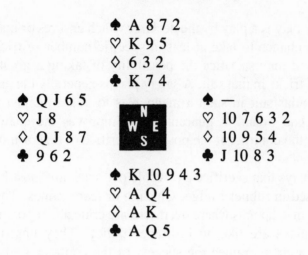

```
              ♠ A 8 7 2
              ♡ K 9 5
              ◇ 6 3 2
              ♣ K 7 4
  ♠ Q J 6 5                ♠ —
  ♡ J 8          N         ♡ 10 7 6 3 2
  ◇ Q J 8 7   W   E        ◇ 10 9 5 4
  ♣ 9 6 2        S         ♣ J 10 8 3
              ♠ K 10 9 4 3
              ♡ A Q 4
              ◇ A K
              ♣ A Q 5
```

Contract: 6♠
Opening Lead: ◇Q

The only possible losers are in trumps. You should lead the ♠3 from hand. If West follows low, play the seven from dummy. This guarantees the contract as the only concern is a 4-0 division. If West shows out, play the ace and a small trump from dummy to pick up the suit with only one loser.

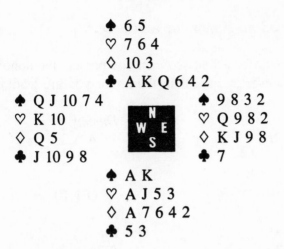

```
              ♠ 6 5
              ♡ 7 6 4
              ◇ 10 3
              ♣ A K Q 6 4 2
♠ Q J 10 7 4              ♠ 9 8 3 2
♡ K 10          N         ♡ Q 9 8 2
◇ Q 5        W   E        ◇ K J 9 8
♣ J 10 9 8      S         ♣ 7
              ♠ A K
              ♡ A J 5 3
              ◇ A 7 6 4 2
              ♣ 5 3
```

Contract: 3 NT
Opening Lead: ♠Q

You have seven sure winners with the long club suit being the best chance for extra tricks. Duck the first club completely (that is lead the ♣3 from your hand and play the deuce from the dummy) to guard against a possible 4-1 division. You are sacrificing a possible overtrick (if the clubs divide 3-2) to increase your chances of making the contract. As the cards lie, this is the only way to make the contract.

MORE FINESSES

When To Lead an Honor for a Finesse.

Lead an honor for a finesse when you possess the honor(s) immediately lower in rank than the honor you are leading.

A. *Dummy*
   ♡ A K 6

   You
   ♡ J 10 9

B. *Dummy*
   ♡ A 4 2

   You
   ♡ Q J 10

C. *Dummy*
   ♡ K 4 2

   You
   ♡ J 10 9

D. *Dummy*
   ♡ A K 6

   You
   ♡ J 5 2

E. *Dummy*
   ♡ A 4 2

   You
   ♡ Q 7 6

F. *Dummy*
   ♡ K 4 2

   You
   ♡ J 7 6

In A and C lead the jack as you have the ten. Lead the queen in B as you hold the jack. In D, E and F leading the honor from your hand is *not* a finesse as you have no future winning cards under the honor you are leading. Remember, to lead an honor for a finesse, you need future potential winning cards below the honor led.

Double Finesses

A double finesse is taken against two missing honors.

A. *Dummy*
   ♡ A Q 10

   You
   ♡ 6 4 2

B. *Dummy*
   ♡ K J 5

   You
   ♡ 6 4 2

C. *Dummy*
   ♡ A J 10

   You
   ♡ 6 4 2

In examples A and B lead toward the dummy hoping the missing honors are with West. In C lead twice toward dummy, playing the jack and ten in the hope West has one or both of the missing honors.

Two-Way Finesses

Most finesses can be taken only one way, by leading from the weak hand toward honors in the opposite hand. Two-way finesses allow you to "guess" who has a missing honor.

A. *Dummy*
   ♡ A J 6

   You
   ♡ K 10 4

B. *Dummy*
   ♡ Q 10 4

   You
   ♡ K 9 3

In A you can finesse either opponent for the queen. In B you can finesse either opponent for the jack.

Double Finesse

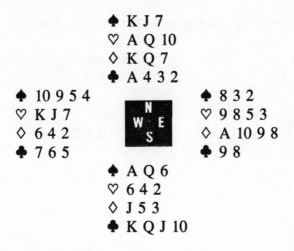

♠ K J 7
♡ A Q 10
◇ K Q 7
♣ A 4 3 2

♠ 10 9 5 4   ♠ 8 3 2
♡ K J 7   ♡ 9 8 5 3
◇ 6 4 2   ◇ A 10 9 8
♣ 7 6 5   ♣ 9 8

♠ A Q 6
♡ 6 4 2
◇ J 5 3
♣ K Q J 10

Contract: 6 NT
Opening Lead: ♠ 10

You and your partner have bid ambitiously to 6 NT and need a large slice of good fortune. Counting your sure tricks you note that you have eight (three spades, one heart and four clubs). You have two promotable diamond winners which brings your total to ten. Finessing in hearts give you an extra chance for two more winners. You hope West has both the ♡K and ♡J. Lead the ♡2 and finesse dummy's ten. Re-enter your hand with a club, lead the ♡4 and finesse the queen. These finesses both work (whew!). Now force out the ◇A and make your lucky slam. Two points:

1. It would not have helped West to insert an honor at any time (you merely cover in dummy)
2. Not finessing would give virtually no chance for the slam

When Not To Lead An Honor For a Finesse

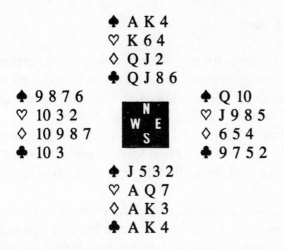

```
                ♠ A K 4
                ♡ K 6 4
                ◊ Q J 2
                ♣ Q J 8 6
♠ 9 8 7 6                      ♠ Q 10
♡ 10 3 2          N           ♡ J 9 8 5
◊ 10 9 8 7      W   E         ◊ 6 5 4
♣ 10 3            S           ♣ 9 7 5 2
                ♠ J 5 3 2
                ♡ A Q 7
                ◊ A K 3
                ♣ A K 4
```

Contract: 7 NT
Opening Lead: ◊ 10

You have twelve sure tricks (two spades, three hearts, three diamonds and four clubs). The only chance for a thirteenth trick is in spades. It would be incorrect to lead the ♣J for a finesse as you don't possess the honor(s) immediately under the jack (in this case the ten). The only chance is to play the ♣A, ♣K and hope the queen is doubleton. It is your lucky day and the grand slam rolls home.

COUNTING

Learning To Count

The ability to count is the real difference between the average and the expert bridge players. The expert has cultivated the habit of counting suit distributions and high-card points and relating this information to the bidding and play.

Counting revolves around the number thirteen. The less experienced bridge player should first learn to count trumps (or in notrump the key suit he is planning to establish). The process is this:

Each suit has thirteen cards. Count the number of cards in your hand and in dummy. Subtract that number from thirteen. The result is the number of cards the opponents hold in the suit. Each time you lead the suit make a mental note whether each opponent follows suit. Each time an opponent plays a card in the suit subtract one from the number of cards they hold in the suit. For example: You have eight trumps between your hand and dummy. Subtracting eight from thirteen (the total number of cards in the suit) you know that the opponents have five trumps. You play one round of trumps and both opponents follow. Subtracting two (each opponent played one trump) from five (the number of trumps the opponents originally held) tells you that they still have three trumps. You play another round and both opponents follow. Subtracting two from three (the number of trumps the opponents currently hold) you now know that they have only one trump left. The next round will draw their last trump.

REMEMBER

1. Subtract the number of trumps in your hand and dummy from thirteen to determine the number of the opponents' trumps

   Thirteen — your side's trumps = number of opponents' trumps

2. Subtract one each time an opponent plays a trump to determine the number of trumps the opponents currently hold.

   Original number of opponents' trumps — one = outstanding trumps remaining

The counting process is rather laborious at first but well worth the effort. It gets you in the thinking habit. With patience and experience more than one suit can be counted. Eventually you will be able to count all four suits.

Counting and Two-Way Finesses

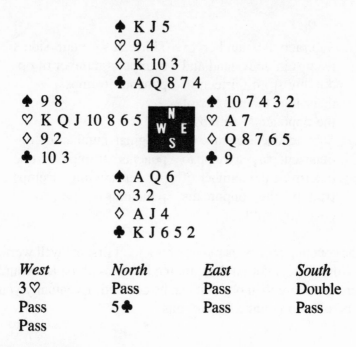

♠ K J 5
♡ 9 4
◇ K 10 3
♣ A Q 8 7 4

♠ 9 8
♡ K Q J 10 8 6 5
◇ 9 2
♣ 10 3

♠ 10 7 4 3 2
♡ A 7
◇ Q 8 7 6 5
♣ 9

♠ A Q 6
♡ 3 2
◇ A J 4
♣ K J 6 5 2

West	*North*	*East*	*South*
3♡	Pass	Pass	Double
Pass	5♣	Pass	Pass
Pass			

Contract: 5♣
Opening Lead: ♡K

The defenders cash two hearts and switch to a trump. You now have all winners except the third diamond and you have a two-way finesse for the queen. After drawing trump, you realize West begin with seven hearts (from the bidding) and two clubs (from the play). You can gain a further count by cashing three spade tricks. You now know that West started with two spades, seven hearts and two clubs. Therefore he has two diamonds and East thus has five diamonds. Consequently the odds are 5-2 that East has the ◇Q. Finesse East for the ◇Q and make your contract.

Any defender who is longer in a particular suit is more likely to hold a particular card in that suit.

The easiest hands to count are those where one defender has a long suit.

CARD COMBINATIONS

A. Missing the king — finesse with ten or fewer.

1. A Q J 10 7 2

    9 8 6 5

2. A Q J 10 7 2

    9 8 6 5 3

Hand 1 — finesse.
Hand 2 — play the ace.

B. Missing the queen — finesse with eight or fewer.

1. A K J 10

    6 5 3 2

2. A J 7 5

    K 10 9 4

3. A K J 10 5

    6 4 3 2

4. A J 7 6 5

    K 10 4 3

Hands 1 and 2 — finesse.
Hands 3 and 4 — play the ace and king.

C. Missing the jack — finesse with six or fewer (if four tricks are needed).

1. A Q 10 3

    K 5

2. A Q 10 2

    K 5 4

Hand 1 — cash the king and finesse the ten.
Hand 2 — cash the AKQ.

D. Missing the king and queen — finesse twice.

1. A J 10 9   2. A J 10 5 4

    6 5 4 3   9 8 3 2

Finesse twice in both hands.

Card Combinations — Missing the Queen

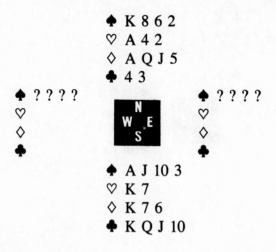

♠ K 8 6 2
♥ A 4 2
◇ A Q J 5
♣ 4 3

♠ ? ? ? ?
♥
◇
♣

♠ ? ? ? ?
♥
◇
♣

♠ A J 10 3
♥ K 7
◇ K 7 6
♣ K Q J 10

Contract: 6♠
Opening Lead: ♥Q

You have all winners except for the ♣A and possibly the ♠Q. It is correct with eight cards to finesse. Cash the king and finesse against East for the ♠Q. If your side had nine cards in the suit, it would be correct not to finesse, but instead to just lead out the ace and king.

49

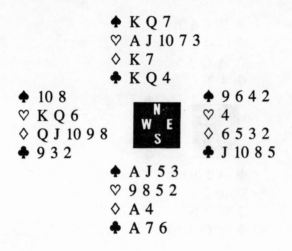

```
                    ♠ K Q 7
                    ♡ A J 10 7 3
                    ◊ K 7
                    ♣ K Q 4
    ♠ 10 8                        ♠ 9 6 4 2
    ♡ K Q 6           N           ♡ 4
    ◊ Q J 10 9 8    W   E         ◊ 6 5 3 2
    ♣ 9 3 2           S           ♣ J 10 8 5
                    ♠ A J 5 3
                    ♡ 9 8 5 2
                    ◊ A 4
                    ♣ A 7 6
```

Contract: 6♡
Opening Lead: ◊Q

Your only concern is two possible heart losers. It is correct
when missing the king and queen (as above) to finesse twice.
Win the ◊A and lead a low heart. If West plays low, finesse
the jack or ten. This lands the slam on the above hand. If West
plays an honor, win the ace, force out the other honor and claim
the rest. If the first finesse loses, return to your hand and finesse
West for the remaining honor.

BASIC PROBABILITIES

1. An even number of missing cards (8-6-4) is most likely to divide unevenly (5-3, 4-2, 3-1). The exception is where two cards are missing, 1-1 now being the most frequent division (barely).
2. An odd number of cards missing (7-5-3) are a favorite to divide as evenly as possible (4-3, 3-2, 2-1).
3. A defender who is longer in a particular suit is more likely to be shorter in another suit. The reverse is also true.
4. Memory aide — The card combination most frequently developed is eight cards (you are missing five cards). These five cards will divide 3-2 about 2/3 of the time and 4-1 about 1/4 of the time (turn the 3-2 and 4-1 upside down).
5. Finesses are 50% to win.
6. Bridge is not primarily a mathematical game. Logic and concentration are much more important. Try to be alive to all possibilities and pay attention to what's happening at the table.
7. On many hands you can give yourself more than one chance. Usually, you should try to break suits evenly first and try finesses as a last resort unless the finesse opportunity is in a long suit.

Cards Missing	Division	Percent
2	1-1	52.00
	2-0	48.00
3	2-1	78.00
	3-0	22.00
4	3-1	49.74
	2-2	40.70
	4-0	9.57
5	3-2	67.83
	4-1	28.26
	5-0	3.91
6	4-2	48.45
	3-3	35.53
	5-1	14.53
	6-0	1.49
7	4-3	62.17
	5-2	30.52
	6-1	6.78
	7-0	0.52
8	5-3	47.12
	4-4	32.72
	6-2	17.14
	7-1	2.86
	8-0	0.16

Probabilities

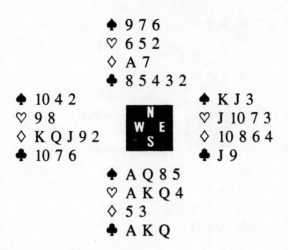

```
              ♠ 9 7 6
              ♡ 6 5 2
              ◊ A 7
              ♣ 8 5 4 3 2
♠ 10 4 2                      ♠ K J 3
♡ 9 8            N            ♡ J 10 7 3
◊ K Q J 9 2    W   E          ◊ 10 8 6 4
♣ 10 7 6          S           ♣ J 9
              ♠ A Q 8 5
              ♡ A K Q 4
              ◊ 5 3
              ♣ A K Q
```

Contract: 3 NT
Opening Lead: ◊ K

The defenders lead diamonds and you win the second diamond trick. You have eight sure tricks and can play for hearts to be 3-3 or take the spade finesse. But you are in dummy for the first and only time so you must decide right now which play to take. The finesse is 50% while the heart break is 36%. Take the finesse.

Probabilities

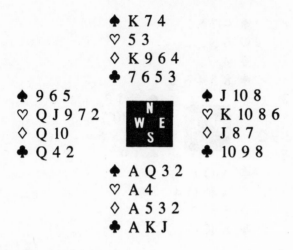

```
              ♠ K 7 4
              ♡ 5 3
              ◇ K 9 6 4
              ♣ 7 6 5 3
♠ 9 6 5                        ♠ J 10 8
♡ Q J 9 7 2      N             ♡ K 10 8 6
◇ Q 10        W     E          ◇ J 8 7
♣ Q 4 2          S             ♣ 10 9 8
              ♠ A Q 3 2
              ♡ A 4
              ◇ A 5 3 2
              ♣ A K J
```

Contract: 3 NT
Opening Lead: ♡Q

The defenders lead and continue hearts. You win the second
round. You have eight sure tricks. You can combine chances
on this hand. Try the spade break first (3-3 is 36%) in the search
for a ninth trick. If the spades divide poorly, fall back on the
club finesse. If you had tried the club finesse first and it had
lost the opponents would have cashed enough hearts to defeat
you. By trying the spades first and then the clubs you make
your contract if either works. On many hands, you can try suc-
cessive chances if you take them in the proper order.

DUCKING

Ducking is intended to conserve entries for the declarer so that later he will be able to cash his winners. The duck can be

1. An essential play to conserve entries or
2. A play made for greater flexibility and safety

You are attempting to establish the following suit combinations in notrump.

A. *Dummy*
   A K 6 4 2

   You
   7 5 3

B. *Dummy*
   A 6 4 2

   You
   K 7 5 3

C. *Dummy*
   A 7 5 3

   You
   K 8 2

In A, B and C correct technique is usually to duck the first round of this suit, conceding the first trick to the opponents. If the suit then divides well, you can cash the established card(s). If the suit divides poorly, you will have the lead and will not have given up control to the opponents.

Ducking

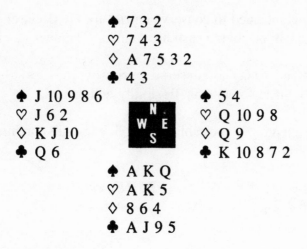

```
              ♠ 7 3 2
              ♡ 7 4 3
              ◇ A 7 5 3 2
              ♣ 4 3
♠ J 10 9 8 6                    ♠ 5 4
♡ J 6 2                         ♡ Q 10 9 8
◇ K J 10                        ◇ Q 9
♣ Q 6                          ♣ K 10 8 7 2
              ♠ A K Q
              ♡ A K 5
              ◇ 8 6 4
              ♣ A J 9 5
```

Contract: 3 NT
Opening Lead: ♠J

You can count seven sure tricks. The most promising source of extra tricks is diamonds. Duck a diamond and win the spade return. Duck another diamond. Win any return and now lead a diamond to the ace. The two remaining small diamonds in dummy are established winners. By ducking twice, you saved the ace as an entry to the long diamonds.

UNBLOCKING

Unblocking is clearing the way in a suit so all the possible tricks may be cashed.

When holding a solid or semi-solid suit between your hand and dummy, play the honor cards from the short hand first so the lead can remain in the long hand.

Play these suit combinations:

1. *Dummy*
   A K J 6 4 2

   You
   Q

2. *Dummy*
   K J 7 6 4 2

   You
   A Q

3. *Dummy*
   A 8 7 6 4 2

   You
   K Q

In each example unblock the honors from your hand. Then use a dummy entry in another suit to cash the suit.

Unblocking is also used to develop extra entries in the suit inself.

Dummy
A 8 3 2

You
K Q 9 4

You need two dummy entries in this suit. Cash the king and queen, both defenders following. Lead the nine to the ace for one entry. Later you can lead the four to the eight for another dummy entry.

Unblocking

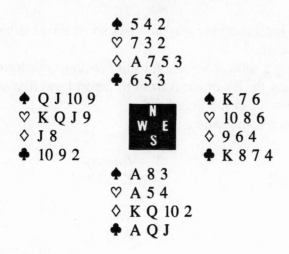

```
                ♠ 5 4 2
                ♡ 7 3 2
                ◊ A 7 5 3
                ♣ 6 5 3
    ♠ Q J 10 9                  ♠ K 7 6
    ♡ K Q J 9       N           ♡ 10 8 6
    ◊ J 8         W   E         ◊ 9 6 4
    ♣ 10 9 2        S           ♣ K 8 7 4
                ♠ A 8 3
                ♡ A 5 4
                ◊ K Q 10 2
                ♣ A Q J
```

Contract: 3 NT
Opening Lead: ♡K

   You have seven sure tricks (one spade, one heart, four likely diamonds and one club). The best chance for extra tricks
is in clubs. You need to take the club finesse but there appears
to be only one dummy entry (the ◊ A). However if you lead
the ◊ K and ◊ Q (both defenders following suit) and carefully
unblock by playing the ◊ 10 to the ace you can create a second
dummy entry in the diamond suit. You take the club finesse
(which works) and now lead the carefully preserved ◊ 2 to the
seven in dummy. Repeating the club finesse lands the contract.
You created an extra entry in the diamond suit by unblocking.

Unblocking

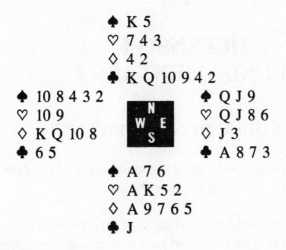

```
              ♠ K 5
              ♡ 7 4 3
              ◊ 4 2
              ♣ K Q 10 9 4 2
♠ 10 8 4 3 2                    ♠ Q J 9
♡ 10 9            N            ♡ Q J 8 6
◊ K Q 10 8     W   E           ◊ J 3
♣ 6 5            S             ♣ A 8 7 3
              ♠ A 7 6
              ♡ A K 5 2
              ◊ A 9 7 6 5
              ♣ J
```

Contract: 3 NT
Opening Lead: ♠3

You can count five sure tricks (two spades, two hearts and one diamond). The clubs are the best source of extra tricks. You must be careful to win the spade lead in hand with the ace (saving the king in dummy for a later entry). You must also unblock the club suit by overtaking the jack with the queen and continuing the suit. By unblocking the clubs by overtaking the jack with the king or queen, you easily win ten tricks.

Chapter 3

DEFENSIVE
FUNDAMENTALS I

INTRODUCTION TO DEFENSE

Defense in bridge is the most difficult aspect of the game. To defend well, you must do four things:

1. Listen to the bidding (partner's and the opponents')
2. Learn the standard lead and play conventions and follow them so partner will get accurate information about your hand
3. Play attention to and interpret your partner's leads, plays and signals
4. Think logically

Defense is difficult because the defenders are working cooperatively and trying to win tricks as a unit. Declarer has the enormous advantage of playing 26 cards (his own thirteen and dummy's thirteen). The defenders must carefully work together to transmit accurate information and then must think logically to achieve the best use of their assets.

Defense at bridge is challenging and fun because every situation is unique and you must think. There is not always a clear course of action. A defender must rely on logic, deduction, intelligent guesswork and signals.

OPENING LEADS AGAINST NOTRUMP CONTRACTS

The defenders' goal when defending notrump contracts is usually to establish and win tricks with the small cards in their side's long suit. This objective affects notrump opening lead strategy. You are willing to give up one or more tricks early in order to develop the small cards in your long suit into eventual winners.

The opening lead is the defenders' advantage in the race to establish tricks. The opening leader against notrump contracts will lead his longest and strongest suit unless information from the bidding indicates otherwise.

There are two stages in choosing an opening lead against a notrump contract. They are

A. Choosing the suit
B. Choosing the card

Choosing the Suit Against Notrump contracts

The following list is the order of preference for deciding which suit to lead against notrump contracts. The card to be led is bold.

1. A solid honor sequence with length

    K Q J 10 4   **Q** J 10 9 3   **J** 10 9 8 5

2. Partner's bid suit (particularly if his bid has indicated length)

3. A five-card or longer broken suit

    A J 7 **6** 4 2   K 10 8 **5** 3   Q 9 **7** 6 4

4. A solid honor sequence without length

    K Q J   **J** 10 9   **Q** J 10

5. A semi-solid honor sequence or "interior sequence"

    Q J 9 3   **K** Q 10 4   **J** 10 8 2

    K **J** 10 9 3   Q **10** 9 8 4

6. A four-card broken suit

    J 7 4 **2**   K 8 5 **3**   Q 9 7 **2**

7. Worthless length

    8 7 6 4 2   **9** 8 6 4 2   **7** 6 5 3 2

8. Worthless shortness, hoping to hit partner's long suit

8 7 6   **5** 3 2   **9** 8

Do not lead suits bid by declarer (unless holding solid strength).

Choosing the Card Against Notrump Contracts

After choosing the suit to lead, it is important to lead the correct card in that suit for two reasons:

1. To transmit accurate information to partner
2. To prevent declarer from winning an unnecessarily "cheap" trick

The correct card to lead from various holdings is indicated below. Remember you would seldom lead from a two- or three-card holding against notrump unless you have sound reason to feel partner is long in the suit.

1. High from solid or semi-solid honor sequences

   A K J 10 3   **K** Q J 7   **Q** J 9 6

2. Fourth highest from broken length

   J 8 4 **3** 2   K 9 7 **4** 2   A J 8 **6** 3 2   Q 10 8 **3**

3. High from worthless holdings

   8 7 2   **8** 6 4 2   **9** 7 5   **9** 3

4. Low from three cards headed by an honor

   A 7 **2**   K 6 **3**   Q 8 **5**

5. High from any doubleton

   K 7   **Q** 6   **A** 5   **6** 2

6. High from an "interior" sequence

   K **J** 10 9 3   Q **10** 9 8   K **10** 9 8 2   A **10** 9 6 4

Notrump Opening Lead Quiz

You are on opening lead against a 3 NT contract with no suits having been bid by your partner or the opponents. Which card should you lead from the following combinations?

1. K J 8 4 2
2. K Q J 10 4
3. A K J 10 3
4. J 9 7 6 4

5. J 10 9 3 2
6. 9 8 4 3
7. K J 10 9 2
8. A 10 9 8 3

Again you are on lead against 3 NT. Partner has bid hearts. You decide to lead partner's suit. What card do you lead from the following holdings?

9. Q 6 4
10. K 7 2
11. A 5 3
12. K 7

13. A 4
14. 9 6
15. 9 7 2
16. J 10 8

Answers:

1. 4	2. K	3. A	4. 6	5. J	6. 9
7. J	8. 10	9. 4	10. 2	11. 3	12. K
13. A	14. 9	15. 9	16. J		

OPENING LEADS AGAINST
TRUMP CONTRACTS

Your opening lead objectives defending against a trump contract are very different from defending against a notrump contract. As the opening leader, you are not trying to establish a long suit as the declarer will trump your established long cards. You are attempting to take and/or establish one or two tricks (rarely three) available in a side suit.

General guidelines for trump contract opening leads:

1. Listen to the bidding. Blind opening leads are for deaf players.
2. It is seldom correct to lead a suit bid by the declarer.
3. Tend to avoid leading aces. Aces are intended to capture the opponents honor cards. Also, do not underlead aces.
4. The king lead from AKx or longer is a very attractive lead. It will usually hold the trick and, after seeing the dummy and partner's signal to the first trick, you can frequently work out the best defense.
5. Do not lead doubleton honors (Kx, Qx, Jx). This lead will occasionally strike a gold mine but usually works out poorly.

As in defending against notrump contracts, there are two stages in choosing an opening lead against a trump contract. They are

A. Choosing the suit
B. Choosing the card

Choosing the Suit Against Trump Contracts

The following list is the order of preference for deciding which suit to lead agains trump contracts. The card to be led is bold.

1. An ace-king combination

    A **K** 7 6 3   A **K** 4 2   A **K** 6

    A K

2. Solid honor sequence

    K Q J 3 2   **K** Q J   **Q** J 10 4 3

    Q J 10

3. Partner's bid suit. With neither of the above holdings, lead the suit partner has bid
4. A singleton, if you want a ruff
5. A semi-solid honor sequence

    Q J 9 4   **K** Q 10 3   **J** 10 8 2

6. A two-card honor sequence

    K Q 7 6   **Q** J 8   **J** 10 3

    K Q   **Q** J

7. A trump from a worthless holding of two or more, especially if both opponents have shown trump length

    9 **8** 3   7 **6** 2   5 **4**

8. A worthless doubleton

   8 6   **5** 2   **9** 7

9. A high card from worthless length

   9 7 3 2   **8** 6 4 3   **9** 7 2

10. The fourth highest card from broken honors

   Q 8 6 **2**   K 9 4 **3**   Q 10 5 **3**

   K J 8 **6** 2

Choosing the Card Against Trump Contracts

As in notrump, choose the correct card to lead within the suit to give partner accurate information and to avoid losing "cheap" tricks.

The correct card to lead against trump contracts is indicated below. You will seldom lead from doubleton honors or lead aces but if you do, the correct card to lead is in bold.

1. The king from ace-king (except doubleton)

    A **K** 4   A **K** 5 3   A **K** 10 7

    A K

2. The top of any honor sequence

    K Q J 6   **K** Q 10 4   **Q** J 10

    Q J 9 3   **Q** J 6

3. The top of any doubleton

    K 6   **Q** 5   **7** 3   **8** 4   **A K**

4. The fourth best from any broken honor holding not including the ace

    Q 7 6 **2**   K 8 **6** 3 2   K 10 7 **3**

5. The ace whenever holding the ace

    A 7 6 3   **A** 7 3   **A** J 9 5 3 2

6. The lowest card from tripleton honor

    J 5 **3**   K 6 **2**   10 8 **5**

7. The highest card from worthless length

    9 8 7 3 2   **8** 6 5 4   **9** 7 3

Trump Contract Opening Lead Quiz

You are on opening lead against a 4♠ contract with spades being the only suit bid by the opponents. What is your opening lead on the following hands?

1.   ♠ Q 8 3
    ♡ Q J 10
    ◊ A 7 4 2
    ♣ K 8 5

2.   ♠ 7 5 2
    ♡ K 8 3
    ◊ Q 7 6
    ♣ A 8 6 4

3.   ♠ Q 9 5
    ♡ Q 8 3
    ◊ K 6 4
    ♣ A 9 3 2

4.   ♠ Q 8 6
    ♡ 7 4 3
    ◊ A 7 6 5
    ♣ K 4 2

Partner opens the bidding 1♠. The opponents arrive at 4♡. What is your opening lead?

5.   ♠ 6 3
    ♡ 7 4 2
    ◊ Q 8 4 3
    ♣ 10 8 6 2

6.   ♠ 7 6 2
    ♡ 10 5 3
    ◊ 4
    ♣ J 10 9 8 4 2

7.   ♠ 6 5 2
    ♡ 7 3
    ◊ K Q J 10
    ♣ 8 4 3 2

8.   ♠ K 7
    ♡ 6 5 2
    ◊ Q 8 4 3
    ♣ K J 7 6

Answers:

1. ♡Q   2. ♠7   3. ♡3 or ◇4   4. ♡7
5. ♠6   6. ◇4   7. ◇K   8. ♠K

INTERPRETING LEADS

Every time a defender leads a suit for the first time, his partner must attempt to interpret the lead.

Leads usually fall into one of three categories:

1. The lead of a low spot card is usually low from an honor(s)
2. The lead of a high spot card is usually top of nothing
3. The lead of an honor card is usually top of a sequence but may be a singleton or doubleton

Again, you must listen to the bidding. Your interpretation of the lead must relate to what you know about declarer's hand from the bidding.

Interpreting Leads

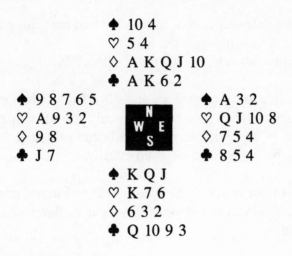

```
            ♠ 10 4
            ♡ 5 4
            ◇ A K Q J 10
            ♣ A K 6 2
♠ 9 8 7 6 5                    ♠ A 3 2
♡ A 9 3 2         N            ♡ Q J 10 8
◇ 9 8          W     E         ◇ 7 5 4
♣ J 7             S            ♣ 8 5 4
            ♠ K Q J
            ♡ K 7 6
            ◇ 6 3 2
            ♣ Q 10 9 3
```

Contract: 3 NT
Opening Lead: ♠9

You, East, interpret the opening lead of the ♠9 as top of nothing. Therefore, declarer must have the ♠KQJ. Realizing there is no future in spades for the defense, you win the ♠A and switch to the ♡Q. This astute defense nets the defense five tricks for down one. Your thoughtful analysis of the opening lead was the key.

RETURN PARTNER'S LEAD

The partner of the leader should give top priority to returning his partner's lead, particularly when partner has led:

1. A low spot card promising an honor(s)
2. An honor card which can be interpreted as top of a sequence

Do not blindly follow this rule. Exceptions occur when:

1. It is impossible to establish partner's suit
2. You have your own establishable suit with entries
3. Returning partner's lead would obviously benefit declarer

The correct card to return is vital:

1. Return your original fourth highest from an original holding of four or more cards
2. Otherwise return your highest card

Partner leads a small spade against a 3 NT contract. You win the ace. Which spade do you return?

A. A 9 3   B. A 9 3 2   C. A 9 6 3 2

Answers:

A. The nine, you highest remaining card
B. The two, your original fourth highest card
C. The three, your original fourth highest card

Return Partner's Lead

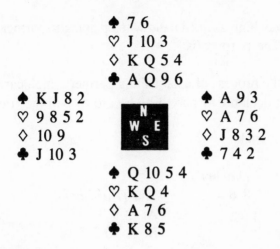

```
                ♠ 7 6
                ♡ J 10 3
                ◇ K Q 5 4
                ♣ A Q 9 6
♠ K J 8 2                        ♠ A 9 3
♡ 9 8 5 2          N             ♡ A 7 6
◇ 10 9          W     E          ◇ J 8 3 2
♣ J 10 3           S             ♣ 7 4 2
                ♠ Q 10 5 4
                ♡ K Q 4
                ◇ A 7 6
                ♣ K 8 5
```

Contract: 3 NT
Opening Lead: ♠2

    You, East, win the ♠A and correctly return the nine. South
covers with the ten and partner captures the jack. He reads your
original spade length as three cards (from your return of the
nine) and shifts to the ◇10. Eventually you regain the lead with
the ♡A to push back the ♠3 for one down. Note that to defeat
the contract:

1. You must return partner's spade lead
2. Partner must interpret your return and avoid erroneously
    cashing the ♠K at trick three

PLAY THIRD HAND HIGH

Generally, play high as third hand when playing to partner's opening lead. The purpose is:

1. To begin the process of establishing partner's high cards by forcing declarer to play a high card to win the trick
    or
2. To win the trick

Dummy
8 6 4

Partner leads the 2

You (Third hand)
A. Q 9 3
B. K 10 5
C. A J 5

With A play the queen. With B play the king. With C play the ace.

There are three exceptions to third hand high:

1. Play the lowest of equals from a sequence.
    In third seat you hold

A. K Q 6
B. Q J 5
C. J 10 9 8
D. A K 3

Partner leads the two. Dummy has two small cards.

A. Play the queen
B. Play the jack
C. Play the eight
D. Play the king

2. Do not play third hand high if it cannot possibly win the trick or help to establish a trick for partner.

>   *Dummy*
>   Q J 10 9 3
>   *You (Third hand)*
> Partner leads the 8   K 5 4 2

You interpret the lead of the eight as top of nothing. Declarer plays dummy's queen. You know declarer has the ace and should play low to avoid establishing the J1093 as winners.

3. If dummy contains an honor and you, as third hand, have a higher honor, retain your honor until dummy plays its honor. Play your second highest card.

>   *Dummy*
>   Q 7 3
>   *You (Third hand)*
> Partner leads the 2   A. K J 4
>   B. K 10 5
>   C. K 9 5
>   D. A 10 4

Dummy plays the three.

With A play the jack. With B play the ten. With C play the nine. With D play the ten.

If the queen is played from dummy, you would play your highest honor.

Third Hand High

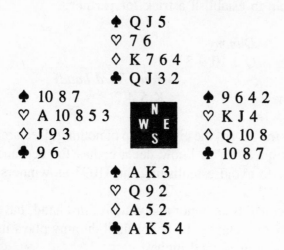

```
                 ♠ Q J 5
                 ♡ 7 6
                 ◇ K 7 6 4
                 ♣ Q J 3 2
 ♠ 10 8 7                        ♠ 9 6 4 2
 ♡ A 10 8 5 3        N           ♡ K J 4
 ◇ J 9 3         W       E       ◇ Q 10 8
 ♣ 9 6               S           ♣ 10 8 7
                 ♠ A K 3
                 ♡ Q 9 2
                 ◇ A 5 2
                 ♣ A K 5 4
```

Contract: 3 NT
Opening Lead: ♡ 5

In third position, you, as East, play the ♡K and return the jack. Your side wins the first five tricks for down one. Your third hand high play wins the trick and prevents South from winning an undeserved trick with his queen.

Third Hand High

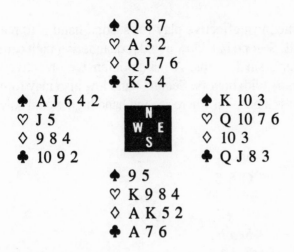

```
              ♠ Q 8 7
              ♡ A 3 2
              ◊ Q J 7 6
              ♣ K 5 4
♠ A J 6 4 2                    ♠ K 10 3
♡ J 5              N           ♡ Q 10 7 6
◊ 9 8 4         W   E          ◊ 10 3
♣ 10 9 2          S           ♣ Q J 8 3
              ♠ 9 5
              ♡ K 9 8 4
              ◊ A K 5 2
              ♣ A 7 6
```

Contract: 3 NT
Opening Lead: ♠4

It is best to play your second highest card when dummy contains an honor which you can top. Save your honor for the time when the honor is played from dummy. You must play precisely the ♠10 at trick one to defeat 3 NT. If you erroneously play the king, South will later win a trick with the queen for his ninth trick.

PLAY SECOND HAND LOW

Typically the most effective play for second hand is to play his lowest card. Second hand low avoids squandering high cards on the declarer's small cards. A prime defensive objective is to capture honors with honors. Second hand low also may force declarer to guess a position where second hand high would solve the problem.

A.

	North Q 6 5	
West A J 3		*East* 9 8 7 4
	South K 10 2	

B.

	North Q 8 3	
West A 7 6		*East* J 10 9 4
	South K 5 2	

C.

	North J 7 4	
West K 6 5		*East* A 10 9 8
	South Q 3 2	

D.

	North K J	
West A 8 6		*East* Q 10 9 7 4 3
	South 5 2	

In all the above diagrams where South (declarer) leads the two, you, as West, do best to play second hand low. In A, B, and C the defense will win the maximum tricks possible. In D South must guess who has which honor. You must play low smoothly to avoid revealing possession of the ace.

There are three major exceptions to second hand low:

1. Usually "split equals" when holding two or more honors in sequence, there is one higher honor behind you and by splitting you assure yourself of a defensive trick.

A.   *North*
                       K 10 4
        West
        Q J 3
                       South
                       2

B.   *North*
                       A J 5
        West
        K Q 3
                       South
                       2

C.   *North*
                       Q 5 3
        West
        J 10 9 4
                       South
                       2

In the above diagrams, when South (declarer) leads the two, you, as West, should "split" your honors to assure a later trick.

2. Do not play second hand low if by playing high you can win the setting trick(s).
3. Second hand may wish to "cover" if an honor is led. (More in Chapter 4.)

Second Hand Low

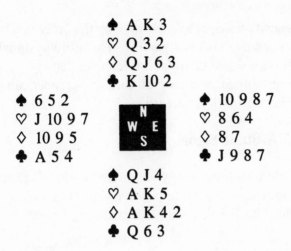

♠ A K 3
♥ Q 3 2
♦ Q J 6 3
♣ K 10 2

♠ 6 5 2
♥ J 10 9 7
♦ 10 9 5
♣ A 5 4

♠ 10 9 8 7
♥ 8 6 4
♦ 8 7
♣ J 9 8 7

♠ Q J 4
♥ A K 5
♦ A K 4 2
♣ Q 6 3

Contract: 6 NT
Opening Lead: ♥J

South must win two club tricks to make 6 NT. He leads the
♣3 and, you, as West, play low. Wriggle as he might, declarer
will now go down. Also note that the ♣A lead would hand
declarer the contract.

THE ATTITUDE SIGNAL

Defenders send messages to each other by the order in which they play their cards. This is signaling. The attitude signal is the most important signal in bridge. A defender can say "come on" by playing an unnecessarily high card. A defender can say "stop" by playing his lowest card.

The Discard Attitude Signal

When unable to follow suit, your discards can tell partner which suit you would like led (a positive signal) or which suit you would not like led (a negative signal).

Defending against 4 ♠

♠ 5 ♡ A K 9 2 ◇ 6 5 4 2 ♣ 9 7 4 3	Declarer draws trumps and you must discard. Play the ♡9. You are requesting that partner lead a heart.
♠ 6 ♡ A K 2 ◇ 10 8 6 4 2 ♣ 9 5 4 2	Declarer draws trumps and again you must discard. You would like to ask partner to lead a heart but have no high hearts to discard. Discard the ◇2 and ♣2. These are negative signals and would, by inference, ask for a heart lead.

Attitude Signal to Partner's Lead

A positive signal is given by playing an unnecessarily high card to partner's lead when you are not attempting to win the trick. This "come-on" signal tells partner you like his lead and would like him to continue leading the suit.

Attitude signals are used when partner has led to the trick or whenever you are discarding (not following suit) to a trick.

Defending against 4 ♠

                    Dummy
                    ♡ 7 6 4

                              You hold
Partner leads the ♡K   A. ♡ 8 2
                              B. ♡ Q 8 2
                              C. ♡ 9 5 2
                              D. ♡ A 10 4

With A play the eight, hoping to get a third round ruff.

With B play the eight, hoping to win the third round of hearts with the queen.

With C play the deuce, telling partner that as far as you are concerned, you would prefer that he not continue the suit. He may still continue the suit if he has the AKQ or KQJ but he will shift to another suit if he has the AKJ or the KQ10.

With D play the ten. Partner has led the king from the KQ. You would like to cash as many heart tricks as are available to the defense.

Guide to signaling

1. Do not give a positive signal with a card that may later win a trick
2. Always signal as extreme as you can without costing your side a trick. That is, when making a positive signal, always play the highest card you can afford. With AK1072, play the ten if it will not cost a trick. When making a negative signal, always play your lowest card. With 6432, play the two.

The Attitude Signal

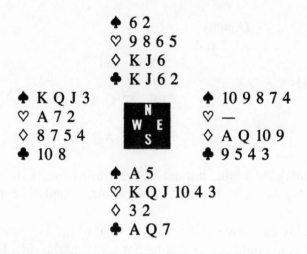

♠ 6 2
♡ 9 8 6 5
♢ K J 6
♣ K J 6 2

♠ K Q J 3
♡ A 7 2
♢ 8 7 5 4
♣ 10 8

♠ 10 9 8 7 4
♡ —
♢ A Q 10 9
♣ 9 5 4 3

♠ A 5
♡ K Q J 10 4 3
♢ 3 2
♣ A Q 7

Contract: 4♡ by South
Opening Lead: ♠K

South wins the spade lead and prepares to draw trumps by leading the ♡K. West wins the ♡A. On this trick, you, as East, have the opportunity to signal and alertly discard the ♢10. West cashes the ♠Q and shifts to a diamond for down one. Without the diamond signal, West would have no clue whether to lead a club or a diamond.

The Attitude Signal

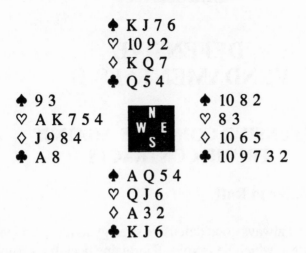

```
              ♠ K J 7 6
              ♡ 10 9 2
              ◇ K Q 7
              ♣ Q 5 4
♠ 9 3                            ♠ 10 8 2
♡ A K 7 5 4         N            ♡ 8 3
◇ J 9 8 4        W     E         ◇ 10 6 5
♣ A 8               S            ♣ 10 9 7 3 2
              ♠ A Q 5 4
              ♡ Q J 6
              ◇ A 3 2
              ♣ K J 6
```

Contract: 4♠ by South
Opening Lead: ♡K

   You have zero points but you play the key role on defense.
Begin an attitude signal with the eight at trick one. Partner obe-
diently continues with the ace and another heart for you to ruff.
Eventually your partner will take the ♣A for down one. Your
partner does not know exactly why you are encouraging or
what you have, but the ♡8 says that you want the suit continued.

Chapter 4

DEFENSIVE FUNDAMENTALS II

DEFENSIVE CONCEPTS AGAINST TRUMP CONTRACTS

Force Declarer to Ruff

It is almost always good defensive strategy to force declarer to ruff a suit in which he is void. Shortening declarer's trump holding will often leave the defense with trump control.

Preventing Ruffs in Dummy

Defenders should attempt to prevent dummy (the short trump hand) from ruffing. Lead trumps when dummy has a side suit void or singleton.

Do Not Give a "Sluff and Ruff"

It is seldom correct to lead a suit in which neither declarer nor dummy has any cards. Giving this "sluff and ruff" allows one hand to ruff and the other to sluff a potential loser.

Force Declarer to Ruff

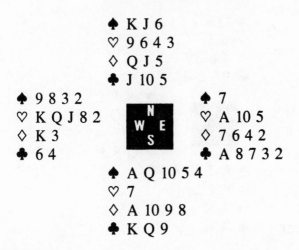

♠ K J 6
♥ 9 6 4 3
♦ Q J 5
♣ J 10 5

♠ 9 8 3 2
♥ K Q J 8 2
♦ K 3
♣ 6 4

♠ 7
♥ A 10 5
♦ 7 6 4 2
♣ A 8 7 3 2

♠ A Q 10 5 4
♥ 7
♦ A 10 9 8
♣ K Q 9

Contract: 4 ♠
Opening Lead: ♥ K

West leads and continues hearts. South ruffs the second round. South sees the danger of losing trump control so he leads the ♣ K before drawing trumps. East wins and continues to force South to ruff by leading a third round of hearts. West now has four trumps to declarer's three. West will take his long trump and ♦ K to defeat the contract.

Preventing Ruffs in Dummy

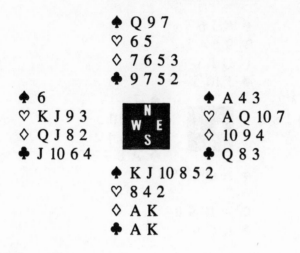

♠ Q 9 7
♡ 6 5
♦ 7 6 5 3
♣ 9 7 5 2

♠ 6
♡ K J 9 3
♦ Q J 8 2
♣ J 10 6 4

♠ A 4 3
♡ A Q 10 7
♦ 10 9 4
♣ Q 8 3

♠ K J 10 8 5 2
♡ 8 4 2
♦ A K
♣ A K

Contract: 4♠
Opening Lead: ◊ Q

South wins the opening lead and counts nine winners: five
trump, two diamonds and two clubs. An extra winner can be
developed by trumping a heart in dummy. South leads a heart,
The defenders win and must lead trumps to stop the ruff in dummy. When you, East, win the second heart and lead a third
spade, the ruff in dummy is prevented and South goes down.

Do Not Give a Sluff and Ruff

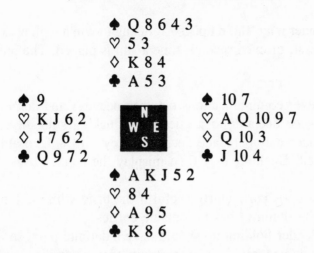

```
              ♠ Q 8 6 4 3
              ♡ 5 3
              ◇ K 8 4
              ♣ A 5 3
♠ 9                              ♠ 10 7
♡ K J 6 2        N              ♡ A Q 10 9 7
◇ J 7 6 2      W   E            ◇ Q 10 3
♣ Q 9 7 2        S              ♣ J 10 4
              ♠ A K J 5 2
              ♡ 8 4
              ◇ A 9 5
              ♣ K 8 6
```

Contract: 4♠
Opening Lead: ♡2

Your side cashes two tricks and switches. On this hand, you can lead any suit other than hearts and defeat 4♠. A heart play would allow declarer to sluff a minor suit loser in one hand and ruff in the other. The "sluff and ruff" would permit South to succeed in the 4♠ contract where otherwise he must eventually fail.

THE HOLD UP

A defender may "hold up" by refusing to win a high honor card the first, or even second, time a suit is played. The purpose is

1. To sever communications between declarer and dummy
2. To force declarer to a guess. By ducking smoothly, a defender may persuade declarer a key card is favorably located. Declarer may then misplay the hand.

Holding up is particularly useful if the hand with the long suit (usually dummy) has no outside entries.

The defender holding up should have a definite purpose in mind. The defender with the opportunity to win a trick by capturing an honor with his honor should usually do so. Hold up only to sever declarer's communications or to force declarer into a guess.

Hold Up Play to Sever Declarer's Communications

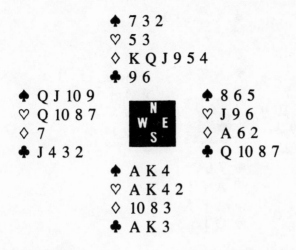

```
              ♠ 7 3 2
              ♡ 5 3
              ◇ K Q J 9 5 4
              ♣ 9 6
♠ Q J 10 9                    ♠ 8 6 5
♡ Q 10 8 7          N         ♡ J 9 6
◇ 7              W     E      ◇ A 6 2
♣ J 4 3 2            S        ♣ Q 10 8 7
              ♠ A K 4
              ♡ A K 4 2
              ◇ 10 8 3
              ♣ A K 3
```

Contract: 3 NT
Opening Lead: ♠Q

South wins the spade lead and attacks diamonds. You, East, simply hold up the ◇A until the third round. South now has no more diamonds and goes down one. If you carelessly win the first or second diamond, South takes eleven tricks. The hold up play makes a three trick difference. Note that dummy has no outside entry or the hold up play would serve no purpose.

97

Hold Up Play to Force Declarer Into a Guess

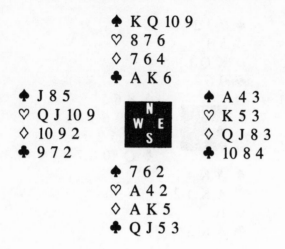

```
              ♠ K Q 10 9
              ♡ 8 7 6
              ◇ 7 6 4
              ♣ A K 6
♠ J 8 5                        ♠ A 4 3
♡ Q J 10 9        N            ♡ K 5 3
◇ 10 9 2       W     E         ◇ Q J 8 3
♣ 9 7 2           S            ♣ 10 8 4
              ♠ 7 6 2
              ♡ A 4 2
              ◇ A K 5
              ♣ Q J 5 3
```

Contract: 3 NT
Opening Lead: ♡Q

South wins the third heart and leads a spade to dummy's king. You, East follow smoothly with the three. Declarer re-enters his hand and leads another spade. Partner plays the eight and South must guess which defender has the ♠A. Your smooth duck has opened the possibility that West has the ♠A85 and you have J43. If declarer misguesses, he will go down one. If you had won the first spade with the ace, South would later finesse the ♠10 and make 3 NT.

DUCKING

A duck is a hold up play used to maintain communication with partner. Just as declarer might duck a trick in order to keep communications open with dummy, the defenders can use the same technique to keep contact with each other.

The usual occurrence is when the hand with the long suit has an entryless hand outside the long suit itself. The defender (usually the opening leader) with the long suit must duck an otherwise winnable trick for the long range purpose of cashing a long suit.

You, as opening leader (West), have no entries outside of this suit. You hold

> *Dummy*
> 7 5

A. K 9 6 4
B. K 9 6 4 2
C. A 9 6 4 2

In each example you lead the four.

In A and B partner wins the ace and returns the ten.

In C partner wins the king and returns the ten. Declarer plays the jack. You must duck in each case hoping partner has an entry in another suit. He will then lead a third round of your suit and you can cash the entire suit rather than just the ace and king.

Ducking

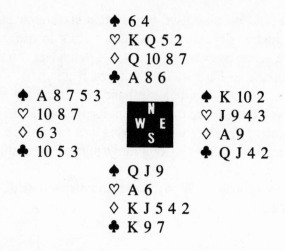

```
                    ♠ 6 4
                    ♡ K Q 5 2
                    ◊ Q 10 8 7
                    ♣ A 8 6
♠ A 8 7 5 3              N           ♠ K 10 2
♡ 10 8 7            W       E        ♡ J 9 4 3
◊ 6 3                   S            ◊ A 9
♣ 10 5 3                             ♣ Q J 4 2
                    ♠ Q J 9
                    ♡ A 6
                    ◊ K J 5 4 2
                    ♣ K 9 7
```

Contract: 3 NT
Opening Lead: ♠5

   East wins the ♠K and returns the ten. You, West, know
that partner has the K10 doubleton or the K10 and a small card.
You have no outside entries so you must duck in the hope partner has an entry and another spade. South attacks diamonds
and East wins. East returns the ♠2 and you can now cash your
long spades. If you had won the ♠A at trick two, your hand
is dead and declarer would take ten tricks.

UNBLOCKING

Unblocking is the play of a high card (or cards) in partner's long suit to clear the way so that he can establish or cash his long cards in the suit. The most common situation is to over-take partner's honor card lead when holding a doubleton honor.

Partner's honor card lead shows a strong honor sequence. You must unblock with a doubleton honor to get out of part-ner's way and allow him to run or establish the suit led.

Unblocking usually occurs at notrump contracts but can take place at trump contracts.

A.
          North (dummy)
          6 5 4

Partner leads   You hold
       K   A 2

B.
          North (dummy)
          6 5 4

Partner leads   You hold
       Q   K 2

C.
          North (dummy)
          6 5 4

Partner leads   You hold
       J   Q 2

A — Overtake with the ace and continue with the deuce.
B — Overtake with the king and continue with the deuce.
C — Overtake with the queen and continue with the deuce.

Unblocking

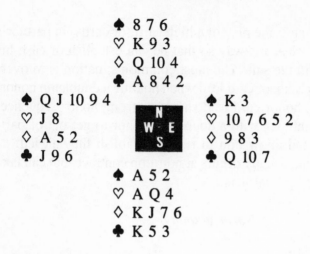

```
            ♠ 8 7 6
            ♡ K 9 3
            ◇ Q 10 4
            ♣ A 8 4 2
♠ Q J 10 9 4                  ♠ K 3
♡ J 8           N             ♡ 10 7 6 5 2
◇ A 5 2       W   E           ◇ 9 8 3
♣ J 9 6          S            ♣ Q 10 7
            ♠ A 5 2
            ♡ A Q 4
            ◇ K J 7 6
            ♣ K 5 3
```

Contract: 3 NT
Opening Lead: ♠Q

You, East, read your partner's lead as high from a strong sequence. You carefully unblock by playing the king at trick one and South correctly holds up his ace. You return the ♠3 and South does his best by holding up again. Partner wins the second trick and plays another spade to establish his long suit. Declarer must develop diamonds to make the contract. Partner grabs the ◇A the first time the suit is led and cashes his two spade winners for down one. The contract makes if East tight-fistedly clings to the ♠K at trick one. Declarer would hold up his ace on the first and second tricks, allowing you to win the second spade trick. You would not have a spade to play and partner's suit cannot be established so that when he gets in with the ◇A, he will not be able to cash his spade suit.

THE RULE OF ELEVEN

The Rule of Eleven is a mathematical calculation which helps the partner of the person making a fourth highest lead to place the missing cards (declarer also may use this information).

THE RULE OF ELEVEN

Subtract the card led from eleven. The result is the number of cards held by you, dummy and declarer higher than the card led.

The Rule of Eleven can be applied anytime a fourth highest lead is made. It is used most often after an opening lead against a notrump contract.

Examples:

Partner leads	Dummy has	You Have
1) 6	1) A J 8 3	1) K 10 2
2) 5	2) Q 9 4	2) A 10 6
3) 4	3) 3 2	3) A J 5
4) 3	4) A J 5	4) Q 9 8
5) 2	5) 6 5 4	5) A J 10 3

How many cards higher than the opening lead card does declarer have?

1) 0   2) 1   3) 4   4) 2   5) 2

The Rule of Eleven

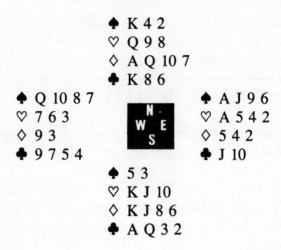

```
            ♠ K 4 2
            ♡ Q 9 8
            ◊ A Q 10 7
            ♣ K 8 6
♠ Q 10 8 7                    ♠ A J 9 6
♡ 7 6 3          N            ♡ A 5 4 2
◊ 9 3         W     E         ◊ 5 4 2
♣ 9 7 5 4        S            ♣ J 10
            ♠ 5 3
            ♡ K J 10
            ◊ K J 8 6
            ♣ A Q 3 2
```

Contract: 3 NT
Opening Lead: ♠7

You, East, read partner's opening lead as his fourth highest
spade. Subtract seven (partner's lead) from eleven and you come
up with four. There are four cards in the three remaining hands
(dummy, your hand and declarer's hand) higher than the ♠7.
Dummy has one (the king) and you have three (AJ9). Therefore
South has no spades higher than the seven. Dummy plays the
♠2 and you underplay partner's seven with the six. Partner
leads another spade and South is down one. If you play any
spade other than the six at trick one, you will be on lead and
you can't continue spades without giving dummy a trick and
South will make 3 NT. The Rule of Eleven tells you that South
has no cards higher than the ♠7.

The Rule of Eleven

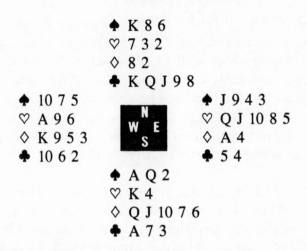

♠ K 8 6
♡ 7 3 2
◊ 8 2
♣ K Q J 9 8

♠ 10 7 5
♡ A 9 6
◊ K 9 5 3
♣ 10 6 2

♠ J 9 4 3
♡ Q J 10 8 5
◊ A 4
♣ 5 4

♠ A Q 2
♡ K 4
◊ Q J 10 7 6
♣ A 7 3

Contract: 3 NT
Opening Lead: ◊ 3

You, East, interpret the opening lead as fourth best and apply the Rule of Eleven. You subtract three from eleven and arrive at eight. There are eight cards in dummy, your hand and declarer's hand higher than the ◊ 3. Dummy has one (the eight) and you have two (A4). Therefore South has FIVE diamonds higher than the three. Your partner led the ◊ 3 hoping he was attacking the defenders' longest combined suit. But you know declarer has five diamonds and to pursue leading diamonds would be fruitless. A switch to the ♡ Q defeats the contract by two tricks. Declarer makes an overtrick with a careless diamond return.

MORE SIGNALS

COUNT SIGNALS tell partner whether you have an odd or even number of cards in a suit. Play high-low with an even number and play low-high with an odd number. Partner can then determine how many cards declarer has in the suit.

Count signals are used when following suit to a lead by declarer or dummy. It is logical to use count signals when following to declarer's or dummy's plays as you would seldom wish to signal attitude in a suit declarer is attacking.

TRUMP SIGNALS are count signals to show partner whether you have an odd or even number of trumps. High-low with an odd number and play low-high with an even number (this is the opposite of count signals in non-trump suits). The trump signal can help partner know if you have a trump remaining if he is thinking of giving you a ruff. This is the only signal ever used in the trump suit.

SUIT PREFERENCE SIGNALS tell partner which of the two "other" suits you wish led. An unusually high card requests the lead of the higher ranking suit and an unusually low card requests the lead of the lower ranking suit. Suit preference signals are used only when you have a choice of cards to lead and when you expect partner to ruff or when leading a card to knock out dummy's or declarer's stopper. The size of the card led indicates which suit you want returned.

IMPORTANT — the vast majority of bridge signals are attitude. A high card is encouraging and a low card is discouraging. Only in the prescribed situations (when following suit if declarer or dummy has led the suit for count signals, when giving partner a ruff, or when knocking out a stopper for suit preference signals) is a signal not an attitude signal. All other signals are attitude.

Count Signal

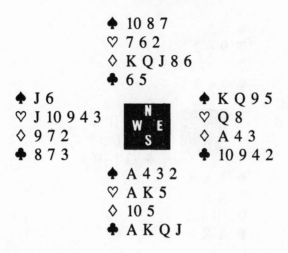

```
              ♠ 10 8 7
              ♡ 7 6 2
              ◊ K Q J 8 6
              ♣ 6 5
♠ J 6                        ♠ K Q 9 5
♡ J 10 9 4 3                 ♡ Q 8
◊ 9 7 2                      ◊ A 4 3
♣ 8 7 3                      ♣ 10 9 4 2
              ♠ A 4 3 2
              ♡ A K 5
              ◊ 10 5
              ♣ A K Q J
```

Contract: 3 NT
Opening Lead: ♡J

South wins the ♡A and plays on diamonds. You, West, show count with the two (starting low-high with an odd number). Partner reads you for three diamonds and therefore declarer has only two diamonds. He holds up his ace on the first round and alertly wins the second diamond trick. This count signal and hold up play defeat declarer.

Count Signal

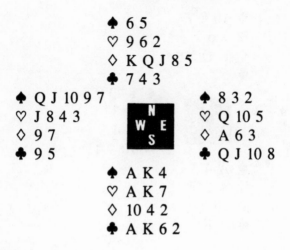

```
              ♠ 6 5
              ♡ 9 6 2
              ◊ K Q J 8 5
              ♣ 7 4 3
♠ Q J 10 9 7                    ♠ 8 3 2
♡ J 8 4 3          N            ♡ Q 10 5
◊ 9 7           W     E         ◊ A 6 3
♣ 9 5              S            ♣ Q J 10 8
              ♠ A K 4
              ♡ A K 7
              ◊ 10 4 2
              ♣ A K 6 2
```

Contract: 3 NT
Opening Lead: ♠Q

South wins the spade lead and plays diamonds. This time you, West, play the nine (starting a high-low with an even number). Partner holds up the ace until the third round this time because he knows that if you have only two diamonds the declarer must hold three. Your count signal and partner's alert interpretation sets declarer.

Trump Signal

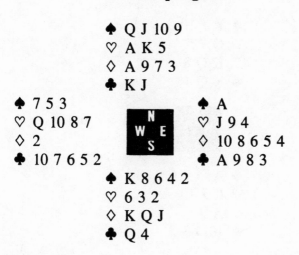

♠ Q J 10 9
♡ A K 5
◊ A 9 7 3
♣ K J

♠ 7 5 3
♡ Q 10 8 7
◊ 2
♣ 10 7 6 5 2

♠ A
♡ J 9 4
◊ 10 8 6 5 4
♣ A 9 8 3

♠ K 8 6 4 2
♡ 6 3 2
◊ K Q J
♣ Q 4

Contract: 4♠
Opening Lead: ◊2

You, East, read the lead as a singleton. Partner gives the trump signal at trick two by playing the ♠5 as South plays trumps. You win the trump ace and give partner a diamond ruff. West ruffs with ♠3 and plays a club to your ace. You know that you can give partner another ruff as he has shown three trumps with the trump high-low.

Suit Preference Signal

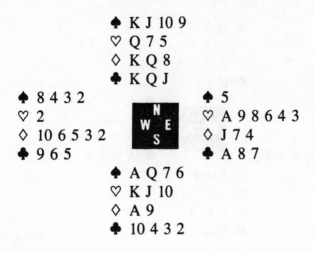

```
              ♠ K J 10 9
              ♡ Q 7 5
              ◇ K Q 8
              ♣ K Q J
♠ 8 4 3 2                      ♠ 5
♡ 2               N            ♡ A 9 8 6 4 3
◇ 10 6 5 3 2   W     E         ◇ J 7 4
♣ 9 6 5           S            ♣ A 8 7
              ♠ A Q 7 6
              ♡ K J 10
              ◇ A 9
              ♣ 10 4 3 2
```

Contract: 4♠
Opening Lead: ♡2

   You, East, win the ♡A and return a heart for partner to ruff.
He ruffs and returns a club to your ace. Another heart ruff
defeats the contract. How did partner know to lead a club rather
than a diamond to obtain the second ruff? Because you led the
♡3 (your lowest card) when giving him the ruff showing suit
preference for the lower ranking of the two remaining suits (ex-
cluding trumps and the suit being ruffed). If you had the ◇A
rather than the ♣A, you would have led the ♡9 to show
preference for diamonds (the higher ranking of the remaining
suits).

Suit Preference Signal

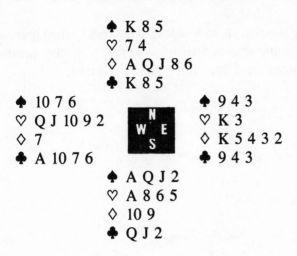

```
              ♠ K 8 5
              ♡ 7 4
              ◇ A Q J 8 6
              ♣ K 8 5
♠ 10 7 6                      ♠ 9 4 3
♡ Q J 10 9 2                  ♡ K 3
◇ 7                           ◇ K 5 4 3 2
♣ A 10 7 6                    ♣ 9 4 3
              ♠ A Q J 2
              ♡ A 8 6 5
              ◇ 10 9
              ♣ Q J 2
```

Contract: 3 NT
Opening Lead: ♡Q

You, East, unblock your ♡K at trick one which declarer allows to win the trick. Declarer also plays low when you return the ♡3 to partner's nine. You now know that partner has both the ♡J and ♡10 and he can lead either one to knock out declarer's ace. When he leads the ten (the lower ranking of his remaining honors) you know that his entry is in clubs (the lower ranking of the possible suits — the possible suits are spades and clubs as it is evident from looking at dummy that he cannot have a diamond entry) and not in spades. When you gain the lead with the ◇K, lead a club to partner's ace and he will cash his hearts for the setting tricks. Note that without the suit preference signal you would be at a total guess as to which black suit to return (as both your holdings and dummy's holding in the black suits are identical) and if you guess wrong declarer will have nine tricks (four spades, four diamonds and one heart).

111

COVER AN HONOR WITH AN HONOR

Cover an honor with an honor as a defender when there appears to be some chance that by covering you may promote a lower ranking card for either you or partner.

A.   *North (dummy)*
                        J 7 6
                                   East (you)
                                   K 9 5
                     South
                     ? ? ?

B.   *North (dummy)*
                        Q 8 4
                                   East (you)
                                 K 7 6
                     South
                     ? ? ?

C.   *North (dummy)*
                        Q J 10 9 8
                                   East (you)
                                 K 6 5 4
                     South
                     ? ? ?

In A if the jack is led from dummy you should play the king.

In B if the queen is led from dummy you should cover with the king.

Both "covers" are made with the hope of promoting lower honors into winners for the defense. For example, if partner has the ten in A or the ten and two lower cards in B, your side will have a third round winner. Work out why this is so. In C the queen is led from dummy and you should not cover. The defense has no promotable cards as dummy possesses the J1098.

Rule — If an honor is led and you are uncertain who holds lower cards — cover. Cover when in doubt.

However, it is almost always wrong to cover honors in a suit where declarer has indicated length (such as the trump suit). Declarer may try to lure a defender into revealing the location of a missing queen in a situation like this:

$$North\ (dummy)$$
$$\heartsuit\ A\ 6\ 4$$

East (you)
$\heartsuit$ Q 5 2

South (declarer)
Leads the $\heartsuit$ J

South has bid and rebid hearts. He likely has $\heartsuit$ KJ10983 or $\heartsuit$ J109873 and is testing your reaction. Be prepared and play low smoothly.

Cover an Honor with an Honor

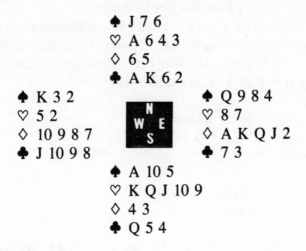

```
              ♠ J 7 6
              ♡ A 6 4 3
              ◇ 6 5
              ♣ A K 6 2
♠ K 3 2                         ♠ Q 9 8 4
♡ 5 2              N            ♡ 8 7
◇ 10 9 8 7      W     E         ◇ A K Q J 2
♣ J 10 9 8         S            ♣ 7 3
              ♠ A 10 5
              ♡ K Q J 10 9
              ◇ 4 3
              ♣ Q 5 4
```

Contract: 4♡
Opening Lead: ◇ 10

You, East, win the first two diamonds and switch to a club. South draws trumps and tries to break clubs 3-3 with no luck. He must now play the spade suit for one loser. He leads the ♠ J from dummy. You cover with the queen (the key play) and declarer wins the ace. South now must lose two spade tricks for down one. If you play low on the ♠ J, South will play low also. West will win the king but the A10 will be over the queen and the contract makes.

THE BEST OF DEVYN PRESS

Bridge Conventions Complete
by Amalya Kearse
$17.95

An undated and expanded edition (over 800 pages) of the reference book no duplicate player can afford to be without. The reviews say it all:

"At last! A book with both use and appeal for expert or novice plus everybody in between. Every partnership will find material they will wish to add to their present system. Not only are all the conventions in use anywhere today clearly and aptly described, but Kearse criticizes various treatments regarding potential flaws and how they can be circumvented.

"Do yourself a favor and add this book to your shelf even if you don't enjoy most bridge books. This book is a treat as well as a classic."
—ACBL BULLETIN

"A must for duplicate fans, this is a comprehensive, well-written guide through the maze of systems and conventions. This should be particularly useful to those who don't want to be taken off guard by an unfamiliar convention, because previously it would have been necessary to amass several references to obtain all the information presented."
—BRIDGE WORLD MAGAZINE

Published January, 1984

Recommended for: all duplicate players

ISBN 0-910791-07-4 paperback

Test Your Play As Declarer, Volume 1
by Jeff Rubens and Paul Lukacs
$5.95

Any reader who studies this book carefully will certainly become much more adept at playing out a hand. There are 89 hands here, each emphasizing a particular point in declarer play. The solution to each problem explains how and why a declarer should handle his hands in a certain way. A reprint of the original.

Published December, 1983

Recommended for: intermediate through expert

ISBN 0-910791-12-0 paperback

Devyn Press Book of Partnership Understandings
by Mike Lawrence
$2.95

Stop bidding misunderstandings before they occur with this valuable guide. It covers all the significant points you should discuss with your partner, whether you are forming a new partnership or you have played together for years.

Published December, 1983

Recommended for: novice through expert

ISBN 0-910791-08-2 paperback

101 Bridge Maxims
by H. W. Kelsey
$7.95

The experience of a master player and writer condensed into 101 easy-to-understand adages. Each hand will help you remember these essential rules during the heat of battle.

Published December, 1983

Recommended for: bright beginner through advanced.

ISBN 0-910791-10-4 paperback

Play Bridge with Mike Lawrence
by Mike Lawrence
$9.95

Follow Mike through a 2-session matchpoint event at a regional tournament, and learn how to gather information from the auction, the play of the cards and the atmosphere at the table. When to go against the field, compete, make close doubles, and more.

Published December, 1983

Recommended for: bright beginner through expert.

ISBN 0-910791-09-0 paperback

Play These Hands With Me
by Terence Reese
$7.95

Studies 60 hands in minute detail. How to analyze your position and sum up information you have available, with a post-mortem reviewing main points.

Published December, 1983

Recommended for: intermediate through expert.

ISBN 0-910791-11-2 paperback

THE BEST OF DEVYN PRESS
Bridge Books

A collection of the world's premier bridge authors have produced, for your enjoyment, this wide and impressive selection of books.

MATCHPOINTS
by Kit Woolsey
$9.95

The long-awaited second book by the author of the classic *Partnership Defense*. *Matchpoints* examines all of the crucial aspects of duplicate bridge. It is surprising, with the wealth of excellent books on bidding and play, how neglected matchpoint strategy has been—Kit has filled that gap forever with the best book ever written on the subject. The chapters include: general concepts, constructive bidding, competitive bidding, defensive bidding and the play.
Published October, 1982
Recommended for: intermediate through expert.
ISBN 0-910791-00-7 paperback

DYNAMIC DEFENSE
by Mike Lawrence
$9.95

One of the top authors of the '80's has produced a superior work in his latest effort. These unique hands offer you an over-the-shoulder look at how a World Champion reasons through the most difficult part of bridge. You will improve your technique as you sit at the table and attempt to find the winning sequence of plays. Each of the 65 problems is thoroughly explained and analyzed in the peerless Lawrence style.
Published October, 1982.
Recommended for: bright beginner through expert.
ISBN 0-910791-01-5 paperback

MODERN IDEAS IN BIDDING
by Dr. George Rosenkranz and Alan Truscott
$9.95

Mexico's top player combines with the bridge editor of the <u>New York Times</u> to produce a winner's guide to bidding theory. Constructive bidding, slams, pre-emptive bidding, competitive problems, overcalls and many other valuable concepts are covered in depth. Increase your accuracy with the proven methods which have won numerous National titles and have been adopted by a diverse group of champions.
Published October, 1982
Recommended for: intermediate through expert.
ISBN 0-910791-02-3 paperback

THE COMPLETE BOOK OF OPENING LEADS
by Easley Blackwood
$12.95

An impressive combination: the most famous name in bridge has compiled the most comprehensive book ever written on opening leads. Almost every situation imaginable is presented with a wealth of examples from world championship play. Learn to turn your wild guesses into intelligent thrusts at the enemy declarer by using all the available information. Chapters include when to lead long suits, dangerous opening leads, leads against slam contracts, doubling for a lead, when to lead partner's suit, and many others.
Published November, 1982.
Recommended for: beginner through advanced.
ISBN 0-910791-05-8 paperback

THE BEST OF DEVYN PRESS
Bridge Books

A collection of the world's premier bridge authors have produced, for your enjoyment, this wide and impressive selection of books.

TEST YOUR PLAY AS DECLARER, VOLUME 2
by Jeff Rubens and Paul Lukacs
$5.95

Two celebrated authors have collaborated on 100 challenging and instructive problems which are sure to sharpen your play. Each hand emphasizes a different principle in how declarer should handle his cards. These difficult exercises will enable you to profit from your errors and enjoy learning at the same time.
Published October, 1982.
Recommended for: intermediate through expert.
ISBN 0-910791-03-1 paperback

TABLE TALK
by Jude Goodwin
$5.95

This collection of cartoons is a joy to behold. What Snoopy did for dogs and Garfield did for cats, Sue and her gang does for bridge players. If you want a realistic, humorous view of the club and tournaments you attend, this will brighten your day. You'll meet the novices, experts, obnoxious know-it-alls, bridge addicts and other characters who inhabit that fascinating subculture known as the bridge world.
Recommended for: all bridge players
ISBN 0-910891-04-X paperback

THE CHAMPIONSHIP BRIDGE SERIES

In-depth discussions of the mostly widely used conventions...how to play them, when to use them and how to defend against them. The solution for those costly partnership misunderstandings. Each of these pamphlets is written by one of the world's top experts. **Recommended for: beginner through advanced.**
95 ¢ each, Any 12 for $9.95, All 24 for $17.90

VOLUME I [#1-12]
PUBLISHED 1980

1. Popular Conventions by Randy Baron
2. The Blackwood Convention by Easley Blackwood
3. The Stayman Convention by Paul Soloway
4. Jacoby Transfer Bids by Oswald Jacoby
5. Negative Doubles by Alvin Roth
6. Weak Two Bids by Howard Schenken
7. Defense Against Strong Club Openings by Kathy Wei
8. Killing Their No Trump by Ron Andersen
9. Splinter Bids by Andrew Bernstein
10. Michaels' Cue Bid by Mike Passell
11. The Unusual No Trump by Alvin Roth
12. Opening Leads by Robert Ewen

VOLUME II [#13-24]
PUBLISHED 1981

13. More Popular Conventions by Randy Baron
14. Major Suit Raises by Oswald Jacoby
15. Swiss Team Tactics by Carol & Tom Sanders
16. Match Point Tactics by Ron Andersen
17. Overcalls by Mike Lawrence
18. Balancing by Mike Lawrence
19. The Weak No Trump by Judi Radin
20. One No Trump Forcing by Alan Sontag
21. Flannery by William Flannery
22. Drury by Kerri Shuman
23. Doubles by Bobby Goldman
24. Opening Preempts by Bob Hamman

THE BEST OF DEVYN PRESS &

DEVYN PRESS
151 Thierman Lane
Louisville, KY 40207
(502) 895-1354

OUTSIDE KY. CALL TOLL FREE
1-800-626-1598
FOR VISA / MASTER CARD
ORDERS ONLY

ORDER FORM

Number
Wanted

DO YOU KNOW YOUR PARTNER?, Bernstein-Baron .... x $ 1.95 =
COMPLETE BOOK OF OPENING LEADS, Blackwood .... x 12.95 =
HAVE I GOT A STORY FOR YOU!, Eber and Freeman .... x 7.95 =
THE FLANNERY TWO DIAMOND CONVENTION, Flannery ..... x 7.95 =
TABLE TALK, Goodwin .... x 5.95 =
THE ART OF LOGICAL BIDDING, Gorski .... x 4.95 =
INDIVIDUAL CHAMPIONSHIP BRIDGE SERIES (Please specify) . x .95 =
BRIDGE CONVENTIONS COMPLETE, Kearse (Paperback) .... x 17.95 =
BRIDGE CONVENTIONS COMPLETE, Kearse (Hardcover) .... x 24.95 =
101 BRIDGE MAXIMS, Kelsey .... x 7.95 =
DYNAMIC DEFENSE, Lawrence .... x 9.95 =
PARTNERSHIP UNDERSTANDINGS, Lawrence .... x 2.95 =
PLAY BRIDGE WITH MIKE LAWRENCE, Lawrence .... x 9.95 =
WINNING BRIDGE INTANGIBLES, Lawrence and Hanson ...... x 2.95 =
TICKETS TO THE DEVIL, Powell .... x 5.95 =
PLAY THESE HANDS WITH ME, Reese .... x 7.95 =
BRIDGE: THE BIDDER'S GAME, Rosenkranz .... x 12.95 =
MODERN IDEAS IN BIDDING, Rosenkranz-Truscott .... x 9.95 =
TEST YOUR PLAY AS DECLARER, VOL. 1, Rubens-Lukacs ..... x 5.95 =
TEST YOUR PLAY AS DECLARER, VOL. 2, Rubens-Lukacs ...... x 5.95 =
DEVYN PRESS BOOK OF BRIDGE PUZZLES #1, Sheinwold .... x 4.95 =
DEVYN PRESS BOOK OF BRIDGE PUZZLES #2, Sheinwold .... x 4.95 =
DEVYN PRESS BOOK OF BRIDGE PUZZLES, # 3, Sheinwold ...... x 4.95 =
STANDARD PLAYS OF CARD COMBINATIONS FOR CONTRACT	
BRIDGE, Truscott, Gordy and Gordy .... x 5.95 =
PARTNERSHIP DEFENSE, Woolsey .... x 8.95 =
MATCHPOINTS, Woolsey .... x 9.95 =

**QUANTITY DISCOUNT
ON ABOVE ITEMS:**
10% over $25, 20% over $50

*We accept checks, money
orders and VISA or MASTER
CARD. For charge card
orders, send your card number and expiration date.*

SUBTOTAL [ ]

LESS QUANTITY DISCOUNT [ ]

TOTAL [ ]

THE CHAMPIONSHIP BRIDGE SERIES
VOLUME I .... x $9.95 (No further discount) [ ]

THE CHAMPIONSHIP BRIDGE SERIES
VOLUME II .... x 9.95 (No further discount) [ ]

ALL 24 OF THE CHAMPIONSHIP
BRIDGE SERIES .... x 17.90 (No further discount) [ ]

ADD $1.00
SHIPPING
PER ORDER

TOTAL FOR BOOKS [ ]
SHIPPING ALLOWANCE [ ]
AMOUNT ENCLOSED [ ]

NAME _____

ADDRESS _____

CITY _____ STATE _____ ZIP _____